AN ABUNDANCE
OF BLESSINGS

AN ABUNDANCE OF BLESSINGS

Ina Pogainis

iUniverse, Inc.

New York Lincoln Shanghai

AN ABUNDANCE OF BLESSINGS

iUniverse books may be ordered through booksellers or by contacting:

iUniverse
2021 Pine Lake Road, Suite 100
Lincoln, NE 68512
www.iuniverse.com
1-800-Authors (1-800-288-4677)

Because of the dynamic nature of the Internet, any Web addresses or links contained in this book may have changed since publication and may no longer be valid.

The views expressed in this work are solely those of the author and do not necessarily reflect the views of the publisher, and the publisher hereby disclaims any responsibility for them.

ISBN: 978-0-595-47842-2 (pbk)
ISBN: 978-0-595-71973-0 (cloth)

Printed in the United States of America

Major encouragement and various forms of helpful activities came from Mary Karl, Randall Paulson, Mary Aylward Stewart, Eve Lewis, Laura Marsden, and Vija Briedis.

Thanks also to the many manuscript readers and their helpful ideas but especially to Sally Clanton, Christine Gorelick, Maureen Hekmat and Mary Donn Jordan.

Special thanks to Becca Kaegi of B-studio for photo repair and layout.

For my Mother and Brothers Andrejs and Max

In Memory of my Father, Brother Juris and
Sister Laura

A man's heart devises his way;
but the Lord directs his steps.

—Proverbs: 16:9

Contents

Bringing the Family to America

By the time I was born in January of 1950, most of my family had survived the War, but it had been a dark and hard time for them. They had spent six years as refugees sheltering where they could—mostly in displaced person's camps in various parts of Germany. Clearly their lives needed brightening and the improvement in their prospects seemed to coincide with my birthday.

Nestled in my mother's arms, I was blissfully unaware of the hardships they had surmounted before I could make my entrance into the life of the family. I didn't know then that they had been in Berlin during the spring of 1945 when the allies mounted a campaign of carpet bombing the city. I also didn't know that they had escaped the city as the Russian army closed in. Or that they had been separated; for nine months my father did not know whether Momma and five-year-old Juris were alive. How they found each other and what happened while they were apart is a longer story for later. Even if they had told it to me then, I could not have understood what they had lived through. It was enough for me to know that I was surrounded by the love of my family. I had no intention of letting any of them out of my sight unless it was time for one of my several daily naps.

To mark my birthday, my father brought my mother a bouquet of white lilacs while we were still in the hospital, but I don't remember that either. I do know that the look and scent of lilacs has always been a favorite.

My birthplace was Trauenstein. Soon afterwards we moved to Berchtesgaden in Bavaria. My mother said it was a beautiful place, mostly untouched by the destruction of the War, with a view of the Austrian Alps. My world was perfect: food, warmth, a soft bed, and Momma's arms and lap. At that time I had no idea how much she grieved for her family left behind in the little country by the Baltic Sea. Or that she wondered if she would ever see her mother again. Since I had just met my parents, I had no concept of such separations.

Most of Germany was in ruins; there was no work for my father in his field of research chemistry. Many people were leaving Germany, so my parents started looking for another place to live too. By that time the Iron Curtain had clanged shut, and they could not return to their homeland in Latvia. My father had been drafted into the German Army in the spring of 1944 while the Germans still occupied Latvia. Although he was a scientist and never did any fighting, he was afraid that since the Communist Russians now controlled the Baltic States, his life would be in danger if he returned there. They also ruled out Australia because it was too far. England seemed too small and probably crowded.

One of my mother's sisters had left Europe; Erna was already in Canada. Papa had heard that there was great fishing there (his favorite hobby) so they thought it would be a good choice. My mother told me later that knowing a family member was waiting for us made the thought of such a journey a lot easier. However, Canada did not want us—at least not all of us. They only wanted able-bodied workers (my skills at organizing and supervising the family were apparently undervalued).

Then my parents started thinking about emigration to America. My family's experience with Americans had been favorable, and Papa had heard that there were many opportunities in the USA. After the War ended Papa worked as an interpreter for the American army so he had many opportunities to interact with Americans. (There were thousands of people in Germany who had been brought there forcibly or who had fled ahead of the Russians. Sorting all that out was a complicated job.)

Papa applied to go to America and eventually we solved the problem of how to get there. A Latvian family, the Briedises, whom we had met in Germany, were living in South Dakota and they had talked their employer, a farm family, into sponsoring us. A sponsor had to sign documents guaranteeing a place to live and providing basic necessities until the refugee family could become self-supporting. We would actually live with the Briedis family, but since they were newly arrived refugees themselves, they could not be the official sponsors.

It was 18 months before I was ready to travel, but it was time well spent. I started by teaching brother Max, who was 16 months older, to fetch toys, keep me company, and dote on me whenever he was awake. Soon I did not have to whine because he would have already found some interesting things to show me: a rock, a little piece of wood, a marble. The two older brothers, Andrejs and Juris, were around as well, but I had not yet come up with a way to employ them.

Slowly I became aware of the other family members and learned that I was special. I had three brothers and Momma encouraged them to look after me. I would beam at them and encourage them as well. I didn't learn my real name until much later. I was called Init, Inina, Inci, Ini, Inite—all diminutive terms of endearment. I learned that my name was Ina (Ena) in connection with some sort of behavioral error. I have always thought that you have to learn the rules before you can change them so I was probably conducting some sort of cause-and-effect experiment.

After interminable piles of paperwork and vaccinations and moving closer to the departure point, the harbor at Bremenhaven, we finally boarded the boat. The *General Taylor*, a converted troop ship, would carry about 3000 refugees to their new homes. The voyage took three weeks and included a stop in Canada to drop off some of them; the final destination was New York.

During the ocean voyage, my brother Juris turned twelve and my parents were surprised that the crew gave him a birthday cake. We learned later that it was something they did for all the refugee children who had birthdays during the trip. I don't specifically remember that cake, but I have found that any situation can be improved by a round of cake for everyone. Perhaps I rewarded myself too often in the years to come, but that has always been a matter of opinion.

My parents gave Jurit (Jureet) a watch. (Everyone was called a number of names, but in order to reduce stress on the reader, I will try to limit myself to one diminutive per relative.) Jurit, who was born in Riga and remembered life before the war, entertained all of us by playing his accordion. He could play anything he had heard, and that day he played music from the homeland.

In New York, a man from Catholic Relief Services (Catholic Relief Services had paid for our trip to America, including to our final destination) met us and steered us through the immigration process. More lines and more paperwork, pictures and finally small photo ID cards were issued, identifying us as "permanent resident aliens." Mine showed a startled, but cute, infant. Now we were ready to continue the journey which would take us by train half way across the country to South Dakota.

I had never heard of the place and had more immediate concerns. By that point in the trip I realized that supervising my mother was a difficult task. Keeping after her was hard since I was so short and her steps so much longer. But I was not daunted and developed a plan. I found that if I slept and napped in her arms and on her lap, she would not put me down; then I would know where she was at all times. In this way, we traveled for two days, changing trains in Chicago, and finally arriving in Sioux City, Iowa, the closest train station to our new home.

Mr. Briedis met us at the station. He had brought a large bunch of bananas for us to snack on during the trip to their place. The Briedis family had been in South Dakota for over a year and Mr. Briedis had been able to acquire a car. They lived and worked on a farm near Vermillion, located in the southeastern corner of the state. So we had to drive a considerable distance before we could finally find a bed. All seven of us had to fit into his car, so I helped out and sat on my mother's lap. Feeling my parents relaxing, I dozed off.

The next day I realized there were a lot of us in the house: five in the Briedis family and six of us. All eleven of us piled into their car and attended a church service that first Sunday morning in America. The Briedis family had found a change of clothing for each of us, so that we could attend the religious gathering without feeling self-conscious. Momma had a new dress and Papa a suit and tie. I had some sort of little dress that brought out my special charm. After brunch most of the older children went off to chat and look around the farm.

I kept Max close at hand when we went out in the yard where our Papa was talking to a creature I had never seen before. Furry and rather large, he responded to "come here doggy" and flopped down and rolled over. My father called us and encouraged us to pet "doggy." I was doubtful at the wisdom of such action. Later I noticed that he would flop down and roll over on his back even when a very small human approached.

My mother and Mrs. Briedis talked all day as they did things in the house like prepare tasty food. I could tell that we were in a friendly environment so I eased up on the supervision. Feeling confident that I would find Momma where I left her, I went outside. I was starting to explore doggy's potential. I did not know how to speak his language—or much of any language for that matter—but whenever I went outside he would appear and try to lick my face. I understood that he was being attentive and seemed to be ready for any mission. For now, I had him just follow me around the yard.

I never learned the full extent of doggy's capabilities because within two weeks we moved again. My father had gotten a job as a lab assistant in the biology department of the local university in Vermillion. We rented a tiny house on Center Street for $45 a month. It was mostly furnished, including pots, pans and dishes. It was wonderful for us since we had almost nothing of our own. Our few possessions had made the journey from Europe in three wooden chests that Papa had made for the trip. Momma's most treasured item was an old Bible, written in Latvian, which she read every day.

Jurit had a nice accordion that Papa had been able to buy in Germany by trading in his ration of cigarettes (he never smoked but he always saved the cigarettes and traded them for things that the family needed). In the chests there were some changes of clothing for us, some stuffed animals, photo albums, a couple goose down quilts, and several green wool American Army blankets. A large aluminum kettle also made the trip and functioned as a bath tub for those of us who could fit into it.

Papa made beds for Max and me out of packing crates that he got from a local grocery store. The big boys would sleep on a pullout couch in the living room although for the time being Juris had the couch to himself. Andrejs, who was six, spent the summer with the Briedis family in order to hang out with his pal Uldis, who was seven.

Our parents slept on the floor in their bedroom on the down comforters. Soon after we had moved in, my father's boss and wife stopped by to see how we were settling in. They noticed that although there was a bed in the parents' room there was no mattress and returned soon after with a spare from their own home. My parents marveled at how thoughtful they were.

Papa was 40 years old when he went to work in America. He had not used his chemist skills for more than six years. He was nervous on his first day and wondered if he would be able to handle the laboratory glassware properly. The fragile glass could crack or break easily. He left early that morning because he didn't know how long it would take him to walk to work. He never wanted to be late. Since I was sleeping in, I missed all the early morning activity.

He would be paid the first of the month; it was now mid-July so we had to get by until then. All my parents had was $4 and they had no idea what that would buy. Momma decided to write to Ernina and ask to borrow some money. She sent Jurit to the Post Office and asked him to stop at the store to see if he could get some milk. Papa gave Jurit a quarter. When he returned he was carrying a quart of milk and wearing a smile. He reported that the stamp had cost two cents and the milk ten cents. He returned the change to Momma.

After work that day, the parents walked to the grocery store where Momma bought fruit costing more than a dollar and then they walked to the dairy. Papa's boss had told him that we could sign up to have milk products delivered and would only have to pay twice a month. The next week a letter arrived from Ernina with $50 in it.

Papa's employment eased our worries, and our lives settled in to a predictable schedule. One late afternoon I went out to check on the parents. They were in the back yard, acting strangely. They had tools in their hands and seemed to be attacking a corner of the lawn. My father had dug up the area and kept turning it over and my mother was pulling up grass and throwing it to one side.

I headed over to see if I could help when I got sidetracked. The neighbor's "kitty, kitty, kitty" was near the fence so I went over to try to make contact. I could just reach it and pat its fat little head before it would move away. When I turned my attention back to my parents, my father was raking rows into the soil which, my mother explained, was a garden. I had never seen her so energized. She pushed little objects into the ground and said they were seeds that would come out of the ground as plants.

Momma's activities usually produced good things, food, something to drink, a bath for me—but about all this I was skeptical. Some sort of conclusive proof would be helpful. Perhaps she sensed my skepticism because she took some seeds and made a little open area by the back steps. She dug a hole and had me drop some seeds in and cover them. Then she brought a can of water and had me pour that in and told me I should water my little dirt spot every day and wait for something magical to happen.

Over the next few days I dutifully poured water on the small bare spot whenever Momma gave me a container of it and reminded me to do it. And then one morning the soil cracked and small leaves were unfurling almost as we were looking at them. In a few more days a couple bean plants were establishing themselves. My mother said in a matter of weeks there would be green beans and we would be able to eat them. My plants did produce beans and somewhat reluctantly I let her pick them and include *my crop* with her harvest. We enjoyed beans, cucumbers, lettuce, radishes, and similar things that matured quickly since it was very late in the summer to be planting a garden. My mother told me that next year we would have a bigger garden with more tasty things to eat.

My efforts to lure kitty into our yard were having some success. The lady associated with the cat was elderly and exuded friendliness and did not seem to mind my attempts. One afternoon she wheeled herself to the fence and stood up with the use of a cane. She handed a big bowl of fluffy white stuff to my mother over the fence. She motioned that the items were edible and in a very short time we helped Momma polish off the bowl. That day we met our neighbor, Mrs. Collar. When Papa came home from work, Momma showed him the bowl with a few hard kernels in the bottom and asked him if he could tell us what we had eaten. He laughed and said it would be hard to determine since the bowl was empty. When he took the bowl back to Mrs. Collar, he learned that we had had our first taste of popcorn.

A few weeks later we also met Mr. Collar, a local judge, when they invited us over for supper. Papa and the judge talked over world events. Judge Collar was very interested in where we came from and the family's experiences during the War. I had a bit of cake after supper and spent my time stalking kitty around their living room.

Mrs. Collar told Papa that she liked children and offered to babysit Max and me if Momma had to walk downtown. In anticipation of such an event, Jurits taught Max to say a few words of English. He encouraged his little brother to say "goodbye my sweetheart" when he left her house. She smiled and laughed so heartily that Max repeated the feat from then on. He would go over frequently and was rewarded with treats and sometimes yelled out his phrase so loudly that you could hear it around the neighborhood

I learned early that it was useful to hang around where my parents were doing stuff. I would sit on the floor and play with whatever was handy, but always kept an ear tuned to what they were talking about. Most of it was gibberish, but after a while I was able to pick out some sequences of sounds that made some sense. So it was that I first started to hear the term "relative or relatives." I understood it would be good to know these people because they would dote on me. My interest was piqued.

Apparently I had quite a number of such relatives, but I had not seen any of them. Aunt Erna, who lived in Montreal, was mentioned most frequently. The next year she would try to come to visit us even though she was not yet a Canadian citizen. She could not get permission to come to America, but she decided to come anyway. Caught trying to sneak across the border somewhere in New York State, she ended up serving several weeks in an American jail. Unable to speak English, she whiled away the time drawing flowers. Soon, someone gave her colored pencils and other art materials; she kept busy drawing portraits of flowers for the other inmates.

Momma found the name of a Latvian minister in the same town where Erna was being held (we had acquired a book that showed all the Latvian ministers in America) and asked him to go and see her. He did that and wrote that we should not worry because she was well treated and was spending her time drawing pictures for everyone around. My father got his boss to write a letter to authorities on her behalf, but it was to no avail; she was returned to Canada. When she got back to Montreal, she had to find a new job and set about becoming a citizen as quickly as possible.

My mother did not know it, but I kept a very close eye on her and was determined to learn her habits and understand her activities. Often when she had a bit of spare time, she would sit down at the round kitchen table and smooth its surface and look around the room. She told me years later that it took a while for her to realize that this was their own place and there would be no more lines to stand in and no more directives to move here or there or do this or that. At the same time it was scary to know that looking after the family in this strange new land was up to her and Papa now.

Life on Center Street

When I was growing up, I wondered how Latvians could know every other Latvian within a hundred miles; word seemed to travel with the speed of light. In the few months since they had arrived in America, my parents had connected with a small circle of Latvian friends in the area. This was a great comfort to my mother since she knew only a few words of English.

When Mr. Briedis stopped by one evening in the fall to drop off some sacks of potatoes and other root crops, he reported that he had gotten a job in Omaha, Nebraska. His sponsor, Mr. Knutson, had given him advice about getting a job more related to his training as a civil engineer and had recommended Omaha since he knew so much about that city. Now that his two-year agreement with the farm family sponsors was up, Mr. Briedis and his family were moving.

I could tell that my parents felt a pang at their departure. They told us to join them. They said that Papa could easily find work as a chemist in that much larger city. My father said, "We will never find all good things in one place, and we really do not like big city living."

I don't remember much about that first winter in America other than one morning we woke up and could not get the door open. The outside world was blindingly white and fluffy and Jurit had to squeeze outside and get a shovel. He dug away enough of the snow so that we could open the door. My mother took extra time to bundle up the small, sensitive ones so that we could go outside and find out what had happened to our yard.

The older boys built forts and tunnels all day long. Max and I inspected their work. My mother made us come in long before our inspections were completed because she was concerned that we would get too cold. As fast as the snow swooped in, it melted and was gone again.

Spring arrived with grass popping up and bushes starting to bloom. The chirping of birds and the scent of growing things filled the air. Jurit had a paper route so he was always busy. One of Papa's colleagues had given Jurit an old bicycle that was his transportation until he had an accident and broke the spokes in one wheel. Our parents ordered a new bicycle for him from Sears and Roebuck in time for his 13th birthday in the summer of 1952. Max and Andrit started clamoring for bicycles too, so Andrit got a bike with training wheels, and Max and I got red and white tricycles.

The new transportation was a delight until some neighborhood gangsters who were about nine or ten years old—started tormenting us. They would watch until no adult was around and then push us off our trikes and take them away. Amazed and at a loss, we took the only action available: we started crying and went inside to report to Momma. The boys soon appeared and offered to "find" our trikes if Momma gave them a dime. They only extorted money from Momma and would not approach if Papa or Jurit were home. After a few of these events, we were no longer allowed to ride on the sidewalk unless Jurit or Papa were nearby. More attention from Jurit was always welcome.

The tricycle was fun, but I still hungered for some living creature that I could bend to my will. We did not have a dog and the kitty from next door was not always accessible. As if the parents could read my mind, all of a sudden a cage appeared in the backyard shed with two rabbits in it. I wasn't allowed to handle them because they could kick and scratch, but I watched them at every opportunity.

Later, my mother let me stand on a chair so that I could look in when she opened the nesting box. Inside, among silky mother rabbit's fur, was a pile of squirming little things. I was not allowed to touch them, but Momma said when they were bigger they would come out of the nesting box into the bigger cage. Then I could pet one.

It didn't take long for them to start hopping around and, as promised, I could hold one and carry it around. Soon, whenever I was outside, I would beg until one of the bigger people took out a small rabbit and gave it to me. I stroked its head and ears and felt the exceedingly soft fur. I studied the small faces and tried to find a way to communicate with them. My mother says that later I was able to pick up even the big rabbits and they would go limp and not resist.

There is a photograph of me with my arms locked around a rabbit. He is facing the camera and is almost as long as I am tall, so it seems it took some effort to hold him off the ground. His expression is complete resignation; mine is glowing joy.

We found out about the municipal pool and started going there regularly, often in the evening after Papa got home from work. The water was warm enough even for me and wonderfully refreshing. Believing that caution was wise in new situations, I would not go in the water unless my mother held me or was no more than a foot away. Many, many years later when she was too frail to go into the Florida Sea on her own, but still wanted to take a dip, my nieces helped me tow her beyond the breakers. I held her as we bobbed in the waves and I had a vivid memory of standing on her knees with her arms around me in the Vermillion pool.

We did not have a refrigerator. We had an icebox which needed replenishing with a big piece of ice every other day. My parents decided not to spend money on ice, so Jurit ran to the store almost every day and Papa would bring home food too. The parents bought a little red wagon for trips to the grocery store and rides for us and sometimes combined the two tasks.

Occasionally Papa brought home a half gallon of ice cream which we had to eat right away because otherwise it would melt. It was sliced into six pieces—some larger than others—and consumed. I probably got more than I needed, but since it fit into my tummy, I figured it was just right.

Without any warning late in the summer, our fine life came to a jarring halt. The owner of our house who had been in a nursing home had died and the house was going to be sold. Buying it was beyond our means so we started looking for another place to rent. Not much was available in Vermillion at that time, and the landlords we encountered did not want a family with four children.

My parents knew a Latvian mechanic who had a car and Gunars started driving them around to places out in the country. Some were so run down that they were not habitable and others were too expensive. The parents were becoming very concerned but kept looking.

A Widow's Warm Heart

Finally, Gunars took them to a large farmhouse where we met Helen. After her husband had died suddenly, she and her two children had gone home to live with her parents. She had seven months left on her lease and she wanted to rent it during that time. After the tour of the four bedrooms on the second floor and the large rooms on the lower floor, Momma told Papa to ask how much she wanted. When she said $20 a month, Momma thought that they had misunderstood and asked him to ask her again (we had been paying $45 a month for the tiny house in Vermillion). Helen laughed and said that was the price and went on to show things that would be included. She left fuel in the basement for the furnace, all sorts of root crops in the garden, chickens and corn to feed them. The house was furnished so we were all set—the only bad thing was that in seven months we would have to look for a new place again.

Papa acquired a car—a 1939 Buick—for $300 and had to learn to drive it. In South Dakota any one over 15 years of age could get a driver's license—no testing required. Gunnars coached Papa, but he drove into the ditch once while practicing, although the car was not hurt. Helen drove Papa into town so that he could get a driver's license; he was very pleased that no one asked him whether he could drive a car. By the time he had to go back to work (we had moved during his two-week vacation), Papa felt proficient enough to drive to Vermillion.

The time in Helen's house was very pleasant—there was lots of room and everybody had their own beds. A large living room with carpeting allowed endless marble games. Wooden block building projects were not impeded by adult traffic. Andrit had started school in Vermillion and now continued his education in a one-room country school. He did not know English when he started school, but picked it up quickly. Jurit had learned some English while going to school in Germany so that transition was not difficult for him either. They brought home school books and Max and I were allowed to look at the pictures under supervision. Momma started studying them so that she could learn more English.

Helen came over frequently to deal with the machinery and to get ready for the auction that would clear the farm of her personal property. She always brought treats, which included cake, so I learned that cake was important social

11

currency. Or maybe I learned that the appearance of Helen meant tasty snacks. From time to time she would pick up Momma and take her to local social events, like wedding showers and birthday parties. Everyone was friendly to her, and in Helen's warmhearted company, it was all a pleasant diversion.

Life in South Dakota rolled along and the parents were hopeful that the future would only get better. But there were times, when Momma thought no one was watching, that a heavy sadness would settle over her. I knew her thoughts were elsewhere. I wondered if the elusive relatives had something to do with her mood. Years later she told me that her family, especially her mother, who she believed was still alive, was always in her thoughts.

She remembered the last time she saw her mother as she was leaving Riga in September of 1944. It was just barely light and they only had a moment because the sound of shells falling marked the approach of the Russian Army. Mimite had come to say goodbye and they clung together trembling and reassured each other that they would reunite when the War was over. Momma was 28 years old as she sat in a small space in the back of a truck with her children. They rumbled across a bridge and watched as the skyline of Riga lit up with explosions in the distance. Momma said had she known how things would go—that it would be 43 years before she set foot in the city again—she did not know if she could have gotten on that truck. She said, "It is a good thing that humans can not foresee their future."

During that winter at Helen's house, there was more snow. For days we had to confine our games and activities to the house. I learned that it was important to share, so I let each of the brothers have their turn at amusing me. On a cold blustery day, Jurit came home with a bundle of frozen feathers under his arm. It turned out to be a male pheasant that had been caught in the blizzard. We were fascinated by his elegant demeanor and wonderfully colored plumage. He thawed out after a few days in a cage in the basement We would sit and watch him, but we were told not to bother him in any way. Once the weather eased up, he was released in the stubble of a nearby corn field.

Just before Christmas, the Collars drove into our yard and surprised us. They handed Momma a beautiful red poinsettia through the car window. Because the judge relied on a cane and Mrs. Collar needed her wheelchair, they were afraid to linger as snow was falling. Momma was very pleased with the plant and even more pleased that they thought well enough of us to seek us out in our country home.

The Christopherson Farm

In early spring of 1953, our parents started talking about the need to find a new place and moving again when Helen's father stopped by for a visit. He said he had an extra farmhouse which he was willing to rent it to us for the same price that Helen had rented to us. He told my parents that when Helen had allowed us to move in he had watched with a critical eye, expecting that windows would be knocked out and furniture broken.

He also underestimated my ability to supervise the smaller brothers who, if left to their own devices, might actually think of something destructive to do. But since they were kept busy looking after and entertaining little Inite, there was no time for mischief. Jurit was so grown up that he was like a third parent. When Mr. Christopherson saw that nothing destructive happened, he was willing to rent to us.

He brought a truck and loaded up our chickens, rabbits, odds and ends, one bed and a refrigerator that we bought from Helen. We moved on February 23, 1953. We came to our new home without looking at the Christopherson farm ahead of time. The yard was overgrown and the house was dusty, but the parents and bigger people tackled all the projects with alacrity. Papa cut and cleared brush and pruned trees. Momma mopped and dusted and organized.

One day all the boys and Papa went somewhere and left Momma and me at home. She got a rake and continued raking up the winter debris into a big pile in a gravel area away from all the buildings. She added leaves and small branches to the heap and then set it on fire. She explained that fire was useful, but had to be watched very carefully. We could not go away from it until it had completely burned up and gone out. Everything was very dry so it did not take long until just smoldering coals were left. Those she raked apart and spread out until they too had gone out. Among the ashes, she found a piece of metal and picked that up with her rake and tossed it out of the way into an old wooden and no longer used hay elevator nearby. Then she went inside to make lunch, but I stayed out because it was a glorious spring day.

What drew my attention to the little wisp of smoke rising from the hay elevator I don't know, but I knew it was not right. I trotted inside and told my mother there was smoke. She tried to reassure me that it was just ashes being blown around and that there couldn't be any smoke. Determined to make my case I persisted and finally she agreed to come out and look. By the time we returned there was a definite plume of smoke rising from the elevator. She ran and got her rake to fish out the piece of metal realizing immediately what had happened and told me to fetch some water.

I got a pail and went to the stock tank and lost about half of it while bringing the bucket over the side. A good deal more sloshed out and into my boots before I got back to the scene. I made that trip many times until Momma finally convinced me that the fire was out. I was reacting to the fear on my mother's face and only years later understood what a calamity had been averted.

The elevator was standing among dry brush near a small shed next to the chicken coop which was close to a barn that held a lot of Christopherson machinery and hay and other important farm stuff. If the elevator had started to burn, it would have been out of control very quickly and probably would have burned down everything. We did not have a phone or a close neighbor, so help could not have gotten there in time. Burning down George Christopherson's buildings would have been a bad start for his new tenants.

When she finally got me to come inside, Momma put dry clothes and socks on me and fed me lunch. Later when the rest of the family came home she told them what had happened. I understood that I had been very good and that someone named God had sent me to warn Momma. I was exhausted and took a long nap.

The farm was a wonderful place. It had a large yard with many interesting buildings to explore and trees and shrubs to hide in. Next to it was a little valley that bottomed out in a shallow creek. Max and I spent long days exploring everything and only heading back to the house when Momma called us for lunch.

When I think back to that first summer on the Christopherson farm, every scene is bathed in soft golden light. We ran around mostly naked and barefoot so that when we had to go to town and be dressed and shod, we offered considerable resistance. Momma found a garment that Max was willing to wear—a striped cotton coverall—and I cried until I got the exact same thing. Loose fitting, it could be slipped on and off easily and had lots of pockets to hold all the important things we found on our expeditions—rocks, bits of wood, empty birds' eggs, feathers, pieces of cows' horn, and odd little bits of metal—not to mention several marbles that had their own special pocket.

One of the buildings was built into the side of the hill that fell off toward the creek. The lower level was meant to house cattle or other livestock and had stalls and doors already built in. The floor above was a storage area for lumber and odds and ends that accumulate on a farm. Jurit cleared an area and set up an old radio. There must have been an electric outlet there as well, but I was not aware of how all that worked—just that one day there was music coming from the strange box.

We understood that this was Jurit's "clubhouse" and we were not allowed to touch his radio but welcome to come and listen when he was home. Jurit could play haunting melodies without sheet music and seemingly without effort on the accordion and the harmonica. Now he had a radio, which was a magnet for the rest of us. The radio provided music, but allowed him to do other things and chat with us at the same time.

I don't remember exactly when it happened, but it seems to me that he is the one who told us that we had a sister who was somehow lost. He wouldn't say much about her, but did say her name was Laura. When I asked Momma, she grew very quiet and said that she had died and I was too young to be thinking about that. Nevertheless I started thinking about having a sister and would revisit those thoughts many times over the years to come.

Jurit had smuggled a couple rabbits to his school and enjoyed the excitement of the other kids who had never seen small ones before. Mrs. Smith, the only teacher for the 13 kids in the one-room school, was also charmed by the little fuzzy creatures. A few weeks later she stopped by our house and brought a small piglet from her farm. Spolite (Latvian for *spinning top*) quickly became a perfect companion. She was a bundle of energy and followed us everywhere, including down to the little creek where we lay around on hot days and splashed in the water.

Spolite would do the same. She had better hearing than we did. When Momma started calling us home, she would get up and start snuffling around and nudging us until we realized we needed to get started. Spolite always got a treat for bringing us back from the wild. Momma told me later that sometimes when she looked for us around the yard and couldn't find us, she would look for Spolite. If she was gone too, she was relieved because she knew we couldn't get lost in Spolite's company.

Tippy appeared in our yard early on a spring morning. He had short, tawny fur, a white chest, and white paws. Deep brown eyes completed his puppy structure. No one knew where he came from or how he got there, but he was only a few months old and willing to be our pal. We bonded with him completely as only kids and dogs can do. He accepted the fact that Spolite was higher up the social ladder and never quarreled with her, but would occasionally lick her nose to show his good will. He quickly understood that he would need to accompany us on our missions and explorations. Whenever we were outside, he was nearby.

Momma said she remembered a scene later that summer and wished she had had her camera to take a picture. She called us home to lunch and up the trail came big brother Jurit, next brother, next brother, me, Spolite, Tippy and a row of ducks. We had all been cooling off in the little stream.

The Briedis family arrived unexpectedly and brought with them two small Latvian boys, Peter and Karl, who looked scared and sad. Their mother had just died and they needed a place to stay until their father could get his life organized. My mother said I was happy to have more companions (she did not realize that I saw prospective minions). Peter and Karl perked up after about six weeks. On the other hand, in every picture taken with them that summer, Max has his arm hooked around my neck and looks grumpy. When Mr. Briedis took them back to Omaha, he left his three children to spend the rest of the summer with us. We never saw Peter and Karl again and learned later that their father had given them up for adoption.

Without being asked, Mr. Christopherson had worked up the garden with his tractor and gotten it ready for planting. Our parents planted a large garden. We spent most evenings weeding, watering, and picking produce that would be part of the daily meals. Ducks appeared after a cooperative hen hatched some eggs that our closest neighbors, the Scholtens, had given us. The mother hen got hysterical when *her offspring* quickly took to the water of a small wading pond that had been made for them. Her calls did not motivate them to leave the water. One day one of the ducklings almost drowned because its down got soaked and it was no longer buoyant. Jurit rescued it and carried it around inside his shirt for the rest of the day until it was completely dry and warm again. He named it Greta and it became very dear to him. It would come when he called and eat snacks from his hand.

A few turkeys, courtesy of the Sears Roebuck catalog. joined our menagerie of rabbits, chickens, ducks, Spolite, and Tippy. Mr. Christopherson came by occasionally because a herd of his beef cattle occupied a large pasture at the farm. They did not need a lot of attention—the big boys filled the stock tank regularly so they would have plenty of water—but otherwise they just ate and lay down and got up to eat again.

On one such visit, he told my parents that they should buy a dairy cow because they could pasture it with his herd and there would be plenty of hay for the winter. He said you have a large family and a cow would provide all the dairy products you could use. He must have told them where to find one because not long afterwards we went cow-shopping. We picked out a young Holstein who had already had one calf and was providing milk. A few days later the farmer who sold her delivered Zimala (zeemala, which means *interestingly marked*) to the farm.

As she came down the ramp, she spooked and bolted, breaking the chain that Papa was holding. She jumped part way into the window of the shed built into the hill. Had she gone all the way through, she would have dropped several feet and probably broken something. Fortunately she got stuck and Papa approached her quietly, talked to her, and got her to back out.

Three weeks later the man who sold her to us came back to our farm. What he saw caused him to put his hands to his head and ask, "What have you done to my cow?" Zimala was on the front doorstep eating sweet corn from Andrit's hand. Her eyes were slitty as she chomped and chomped, juice running down her jaw, not restrained in any way. Watching Zimala eat, I decided that sweet corn must be cake to a cow.

The farmer gave my parents $50 because he said he had overcharged them (they had paid $250). He said Mr. Knutson, the farmer who had sponsored us, had told him where we had come from and that our resources were very limited. My parents marveled over this event, and my mother decided it was another example of the kind hearts living in South Dakota.

Zimala had a sweet personality. She was very patient and would stop her grazing wherever she happened to be when approached for milking time. She would stand quietly until my mother was done and then go back to work on the grass. She would not flick an ear at us crawling underneath or hanging on her neck. She learned Latvian very quickly and soon understood that *maja, maja* meant that she should come home. She was a cornucopia of dairy products—homemade cheese, yogurt, cottage cheese, butter, fresh sweet milk, and fluffy whipped cream to go with the strawberries from the garden.

During an evening it started to rain and just before dawn my mother was awakened by the bellowing of cattle. She got up and went outside to see what the problem might be. Through the mist she could make out the Christopherson herd on the other side of the creek all bunched up against the fence. The creek had vanished and in its place was a lake! She ran back inside to wake Papa who found her story hard to believe but dressed and came outside and was astonished to see that she was right.

As they were deciding what to do, Mr. Christopherson drove in the yard and told them to come down the road and get Zimala because he was going to open a gate to let his herd into another pasture on higher ground. My parents called *maja, maja.* Zimala separated herself from the rest and followed them home along the road and over the bridge that crossed the now rushing little river.

By the time I got up, Zimala was staked out near the barn in tall grass and our parents told us what had happened. After breakfast they drove into town, leaving all the Briedis children and us in Jurit's custody. In a very short time, he had dragged out an old door, some barrels, pieces of lumber and rope and fashioned a raft on the edge of our new lake. He also found some long poles for steering and moving the raft—the smaller one he gave to Andrit.

The Briedis children would not get on board because their older sister Vija thought it was not safe. The rest of us would follow Jurit anywhere, so he helped us up and pushed off. Max and I sat on the edge splashing our feet in the water, reveling in the light sparkling off the ripples. Tippy barked and ran alongside and then lay down waiting for us to come back to shore. I don't know how long we were out there, but it was a really fine time.

Jurit was very careful not to let us get into the current because that could have swept us downriver, but his caution did not alleviate the distress on our parents' faces when they came home and saw where we were. Our boating event was soon over. By the next day the lake had shrunk and we could make out the creek bed again. But the memory of that morning has stayed. When I thought about it much later, I realized that sometimes calculated risks lead to a real adventure. But it is even better if someone else does all the calculations and makes the raft.

My parents and big brother lived parallel lives that were not spent lolling about in the little creek or on rambling hikes around the farm. Andrit, often lost in a book, would not always hear when he was called, but we usually knew where to find him. He spent a lot of time with Uldis and Janis doing bigger-boy stuff that summer. He had to feed the rabbits and make sure that they had fresh water. The boys raked up dried grass that Papa had cut for bedding for the rabbits and Spolite and for food for Zimala.

Papa went to work every weekday and on weekends worked to make life around the house easier. He bought a new gas stove for Momma and arranged to have a metal container made with a faucet at the bottom that could be set on the old stove in the kitchen. It acted as our hot water heater. Outside, Mr. Christopherson had set up a tank in a tree which would heat up during the day so that warm showers were available. With that water, Papa would fill the canvas collapsible bath tub for anyone who wanted a leisurely soak. Since we had no close neighbors and few visitors, we had a sense of total freedom and security at our wild little place in the country.

The grownups thought that when we were outside we were just "playing," but our hikes around the farm were not totally aimless. Soon Max and I had various construction projects started wherever raw material was available. Along the sandy edge of the driveway we built roads that often had to be rebuilt because car traffic tended to obliterate them. Elsewhere we used sticks and boards to build small houses which sometimes disappeared into the stove for kindling. The adults had trouble seeing our projects as clearly as we did. One day Max and I crossed the little creek and trudged up to a rock pile we had noticed before. It had many smooth round rocks that were small enough to be handled easily. We had decided to build a fort closer to the creek.

So we rolled down a bunch of rocks for that purpose and when I thought we had enough I went down to lay out the parameters of our fort. Max kept finding more good rocks and one almost hit me as it came down the hill, so I told him to stop rolling and come down to help me. After a pause another couple rocks came down and although I ducked, one hit me square in the shoulder. I fell over and it was a while before I could get up. Max came running down the hill and kept saying how sorry he was and would I please not tell Momma.

When we went home, I realized I could not lift my arm. It didn't take long for Momma to notice. She asked what had happened. I told her that I fell down. I had decided not to overwhelm Momma with too many details. If she gave Max a strong talking to, he would be grumpy and I would still have a sore shoulder. My plan resulted in Momma fussing over me for the next couple days until it was clear that my arm was getting better.

Max was grateful that he had not been reported, so he was available for many additional tasks. For instance, he was sent into the kitchen when no one was there to pilfer an extra piece of *plats maize* for me—a kind of coffee cake but more substantial and less sweet than what Americans eat. Now that we had a refrigerator, food storage was much easier. It also meant that snacks and leftover cake could be found in there as well. After several days of catering to my whims, he said he was tired of being a *vergs* (slave) so I let up on the demands but would remind him of this incident from time to time when it was most useful for me to do so.

Although our parents were familiar with the animals that inhabited their native country, America had many others they had never seen before. One summer afternoon a small black-and-white striped creature lumbered slowly around the yard, eventually going into the basement through a ground-level window. Its demeanor said it wasn't afraid of anyone, so the parents wondered what it could be and if it were dangerous. When Papa asked his colleagues in the biology department, they told him it was a skunk. They warned that we should not agitate it in any way because it could spray a dreadful smelling liquid that would make our whole house uninhabitable. So, we all paid attention to that advice. After a day or so, it went away.

On another occasion, Tippy's excited barking alerted us to a huge prehistoric-looking animal in the yard. It was an enormous snapping turtle. Papa used ice tongs to pick it up by its shell to keep out of range of its reaching head and snapping jaws. Everyone wondered how it got to our yard since the little creek was too shallow to shelter it. Our parents decided it could be dangerous to small animals and small children. So Momma took a picture and then Papa put it in the trunk of the car and he and Jurit drove it to the Vermillion River and let it go.

As far as I was concerned, life on the Christopherson farm was complete. I thought I would probably live there forever. But Papa learned that there was little future for him in Vermillion since the university did not have a chemistry department. The lab assistant's salary would not increase much beyond the $300 a month that he was earning. He was told that his best opportunities were going to be in industry, so he started looking for a new job. Over the next two years he traveled to Cleveland, Chicago, and Minneapolis, but all the job possibilities were in the heart of the cities and would require going back to urban living. He found that hard to contemplate. Momma reminded him of all the animals we had acquired and wondered what would we do with them. So he kept looking. We were not told much about the search because they thought there was little point in worrying the small wild people.

It was probably the Fourth of July when we went to Vermillion and saw a parade with marvelous wagons and cars and fire trucks. Max ran around picking up the candy that was thrown to the sidewalk. I got my cut from his efforts, and when I told him my shoulder still had a twinge, he gave me another handful. I cached my treats in the deep pockets of my coveralls and extracted a piece to eat.

All of a sudden my perception of the world changed forever with the clip-clop of shod hoofs on the pavement and the most amazing creatures came down the street. Golden horses with flaxen manes pranced past us. Their ornate bridles and saddles jingled with metal decorations. I stared and stopped chewing my candy. From that point on I tried to learn everything I could about horses and constantly asked my mother if it wouldn't be best if we had one too.

Now I noticed them everywhere: during car trips to town or when we visited friends or went to our Latvian church services. I scanned the fields for a glimpse of a horse or pony. I brought up the subject when we were alone so that I could have Momma's full attention. When we were out in the yard or the garden or when she was tucking me in at night. But she was not easily persuaded. She said horses are hard to handle and need a lot of food.

I had also scoped out ponies and asked if I could have a pony. How about a small pony? She said we would discuss it when I was older but in the meantime she would tell me a story about horses she knew from her childhood. I was instantly appeased because I loved her stories.

It is winter. I am nine years old and my father has to go to Riga. The train stops at Jaunskalsnavas station which is about seven kilometers from our home. I have to accompany him to Aiviekstes ferry crossing and then he will go the rest of the way on foot. The older siblings who had to do the heavy work on the farm were not taken on these trips since there only needed to be someone to hold the reins on the way home. It was a job that I had done before. My old friend Ansis is already hitched to the sled and he has made many such trips and is calm and easy for children to handle.

The night is bright and quiet while the moon seems to peek out from the clouds and then hide again. I think it is playing with us, but my father says that the clouds are passing in front of the moon. No matter, I am snug and warm sitting next to him on a sack filled with straw, and I am content. The sled creaks but Ansis' steps are muffled. We come to a forest where large fir trees line the track on both sides, their branches weighed down with snow. I turn to watch as the trees slide by—they are so tall and dignified. I wonder about the small birds and squirrels that have taken shelter in their branches. I, too, am safe and warm.

At Aieviekstes my father gets out. He turns Ansis homeward and then tucks me in with his old sheepskin coat. He hands me the reins and says "Now, little one, you can go home. Ansis knows the way home just don't let go of the reins." I had heard all that before, but my father always reminds me that Ansis can be trusted to find his way home. He needs no encouragement and his easy trot soon brings us back to the forest. The tall firs envelop the horse and sled and the only sound is the creaking and swishing of the runners. The night is still and I cannot keep my eyes open. The sled has a flat, open bed filled with straw. I don't think that I can sit up. I just want to lie down.

I start awake when the horse is making a turn. This track does not look familiar so I pull the reins and try to turn him the other way. He does not want to go, but I insist and he slowly moves along the path I have chosen. Soon the going gets harder for him and the sled does not move as easily as it did. I realize we are sinking into deep snow. My heart is starting to pound and then sensible Ansis stops because he can go no farther.

My father's words ring in my ear: "Just hold the reins, Ansis knows the way." I climb down from the sled and start to shiver. I have driven us onto a narrow footpath and now I must turn the sled around without breaking something or turning it over. I don't know where I am and my teeth are chattering. Ansis is standing quietly waiting for instructions. I decide to do what I have seen my father do. I

take hold of his bridle and turn him a little to the left and urge him to back up and
then forward a little to the right and then back again. We back and turn and back
and turn until finally we are headed back the way we came.
*   I feel such joy and scramble back into the sled and pull the sheepskin coat*
around me. I hold the reins, but don't give Ansis any more directions. My fearful
shivering subsides. The next thing I know Ansis has stopped by the barn and my
oldest brother has come out to unhitch him and put him inside for the night.

I had questions for her about the farm horses of her childhood and her father.
She told me that he died in 1946; she is sorry that I will not be able to meet my
Grandfather. All these stories about relatives, yet they continued to be out of my
reach and beyond the circle of my influence. Momma's story has successfully distracted me from nagging her about a pony and I think about the sled ride in the
winter night as she tucks me into bed.

Mr. Christopherson painted our house and brought wallpaper so we could fix
up the inside. He also installed a new wood furnace for us. It sat in the living
room and would warm the house from there. When we moved in, Mr. Christopherson cautioned us that there were bees living inside the north wall of our
house. We were all warned and thought nothing more about it. He was a kind
and thoughtful landlord and noticed things we needed before we did. One day he
came by and offered Jurit a job driving a tractor for various farm duties at his
place. Jurit jumped at the opportunity so he was gone to work for many days that
summer. He came home looking brown and then browner—he was the only one
of the kids who developed a really nice tan.

Jurit continued to work for the Christophersons that summer as he was hoping to save up enough money so that he could buy a car. The next summer when
he was 15 he also worked for the Scholtens. Their son Harry was in his class. He
did all sorts of farm work including helping string barbed wire fences—dangerous work. The wire was nailed at one post and then stretched tightly beyond the
next post so it could be nailed again.

Mr. Scholten had modified the back of his tractor so that he could put a whole
roll on it and slowly unwind the barbed wire while stretching it. One day the wire
broke while Jurit was moving it closer to a post. The barbed wire cut several fingers of his right hand to the bone. Mr. Scholten took him to the hospital right
away and brought him home with his hand stitched up and bandaged. Jurit felt
poorly for several days and stayed upstairs where he read comic books and
napped.

Around that time we awoke to find the screen door covered with enraged bees.
We were trapped inside until the evening or very early morning. The adults went

out from time to time, but the rest of us were confined to the house unless we covered ourselves with a blanket. On one trip outside, Andrit was stung several times in his ear. It swelled up and leaned over so it looked like it was broken. After a few days of the siege, Jurit drove us in to town to the pool during the day hoping that the bees would get over whatever it was that they were mad about. But to no avail. Finally Papa had to buy poison and spray them with it at night.

When he got close enough to do that, he reported that the tree trunk close to the house and the wall around the bee hive smelled like pee. The boys were confronted and Andrit who was nine and five-year-old Max confessed that since the injured Jurit was not able to carry out the overnight pee pail, they had decided to take a short cut and started pouring it out the window. The window was right above the place where the bees were living. They stopped doing that and the bees that were left calmed down and life went back to normal. The parents felt bad about the whole situation so they smeared honey on the wall and around the opening to the bee's home as a token of reconciliation. The bees ate the honey and never bothered us again.

Summer Ends

But I am getting ahead of the story because the first summer on the Christopher-son farm is not over. With the Briedis children spending the summer with us we got used to having a big family. There is a photograph with all of us inside the stock tank cooling off and another one of Janis and Uldis using a leafy branch to drive the flies off Zimala while she was grazing. Not a vital task, but it kept the boys occupied for a while. Momma liked to take pictures with a camera that she bought in Germany so there is an extensive record of life in the country.

Spolite's freedom came to an end when she discovered the garden and lost interest in expeditions around the farm. Young carrots, beets and new potatoes called to her, and no amount of chastising language could alter her intentions. Papa made a pen and at night Spolite was confined to a stall in the lower level of the animal barn. Her stall was bedded with dried grass or straw and she would push a huge pile together into one corner. She would move it around until she was satisfied with her nest and then would snuggle down and become almost invisible. Another corner was her bathroom because pigs are very tidy if they have room to maneuver.

The poultry also had pens and small buildings for nighttime shelter. The ducks had enjoyed padding down to the creek every day, but when Jurit's favorite Greta disappeared and the next day another duck disappeared, they were con-fined to their fenced-in area. Jurit walked the fields and the edge of the creek call-ing for Greta, but found no sign of her. The remaining ducks were not happy and milled around the gate to their yard and complained for several days before they got used to the new arrangement. Max and I noted their discontent but how could you explain to a duck that a fox or coyote was planning to have it for lunch?

Momma fed the animals first thing in the morning before she had any break-fast. She also collected the eggs. We helped look for them because the hens would hide them in an effort to brood a family. I knew that they were important, but I did not make a connection between the fluctuating numbers of roosters, rabbits, and turkeys and the wonderful roasts, stews, and soups that appeared in the kitchen. The parents were very careful to shelter us from the process of converting farm stock to food.

Our main companion continued to be Tippy and a finer friend would have been hard to find. He accompanied us all around the farm and when we crawled under some bushes—our "cave" to escape the heat of the day—Tippy would join us and be our pillow. With our heads on his soft side, he was probably hot but he never complained. In this way Max and I spent whole afternoons chatting and watching what went on in the yard. We liked the thought of being hidden, but whenever Momma called him, Tippy would immediately go to her, revealing our location. Although he was our pal, he knew who was in charge of the pack and where all his buttered bread came from.

It always pleased me to see the animals eat their food, so Momma often would let me take something to them. For Tippy it was table scraps or if nothing else was around she would smear lard on a piece of bread and let me give that to him. He took it carefully from my hand and lay down to consume it. A couple bites and it was gone. Zimala craved sweet corn or any cob of corn when the garden season was over. She also liked bread and would vacuum a slice or two off your hand so that you had to be careful that the hand did not go too.

Spolite ate her food as if every meal was a feast. She would get a big pail of scraps, boiled potatoes, whey or other dairy byproducts. Leaves left over from the daily garden activities were also included. Turnip, beet, and carrot tops and the outside leaves from cabbages were great favorites. She would close her eyes and seem to hum to herself as she slurped up the contents of her trough. I was too small to carry that pail but went along to facilitate the process. When I got back from such exertions, I would beg a treat from Momma. I had noticed that snaring snacks was easier when I had done something helpful. Sometimes just reporting my presence in the vicinity of useful work was enough to get a reward.

Some Sundays we traveled a distance to a gathering of Latvians where a church service was held in the home language. Most Latvians were Lutherans. Although there were many Lutheran churches in South Dakota, my parents preferred the ones that Momma could understand. Momma said I was always grumpy when she dressed me for church in a little dress and nice shoes and braided my hair. But I loved the singing and although I tried to pay attention to the sermon, I was soon daydreaming about horses and the adventures I would have once I had a horse. Afterwards there were social gatherings with potluck lunches and always some cake. I found it was best to start and end my lunch with cake.

Latvian services were not held every week so on the rest of the Sundays the parents read to us from the Bible and told stories that they thought we could understand. Sunday was always a day of rest; only vital tasks like feeding the animals and ourselves were allowed. The parents often took a nap on Sunday afternoon. Usually we went outside so as not to disturb them unless we were also napping—one of my preferred activities. But Max was usually restless and would wake me so that I would come outside with him to do some exploring or just sit under our bushes and chat. Max was always chatting. I remember the sound of his voice was soothing.

Preparing enough food for their four children and the three Briedis children took up a lot of time and effort on Momma's part. Papa helped too. One thing he liked to do was fish; in fact he loved to fish; and the rest of us loved to eat the fish he caught. He never used bait but, instead, he used small spinning lures that he made himself from mother of pearl or copper. They moved very lightly and flashed in the water. If there was a northern or bass around it would usually succumb. He also caught carp, considered rough and not edible by the local population, but we ate them anyway. Carp living in clean water are tasty, but do have a lot of bones and some that are so small they are hard to see. Momma would always pick apart the fish and remove the bones before she would give any to Max and me. She would not let us do it ourselves because she didn't trust us to be thorough enough.

On a fishing expedition that summer, Papa took Max and me along when we promised to play quietly on the bank of the river and not interfere with his casting. We were good for a very long time, but as the day was waning, we started rolling down the bank in the tall grass and couldn't help giggling. Papa told us to go back to the car. He said he would be there soon.

We headed to the car across a hayfield when we heard the *hoo-hoo* of an owl and then the shadow of an enormous bird passed overhead. Max ran up behind me and tackled me and covered me with his body. I was annoyed until I realized that he was offering himself to be eaten first. Our hearts pounding, we lay without moving, and soon Max said to get up and run a zigzag pattern to the car. He pulled open the door and we tumbled inside and huddled on the back seat. The next thing I remember is Papa pulling into our yard and then being carried into the house. Momma had supper ready. We were famished.

Sunday afternoons we went visiting or we received visitors. The Pilag family worked on a farm and had invited us to come to see their place. There was the usual Latvian buffet lunch with a bit of cake to tide me over until later when there would be coffee and cake for the adults and more cake for me.

In between, Max and I went outside to look around the property. Max was interested in their duck pond and wanted to know whether there might be some fish in it. I wandered into their barn because the animals were always my interest. Most farms had cats that were usually half wild and could not be picked up and petted. But that day a white, pudgy tomcat came over and wound his way around my legs while purring vigorously. I picked him up (it took two tries to get him off the ground) but he did not protest. I carried him to the house and told Momma, "Look what I found." Momma explained that he was a nice cat, but he belonged to the Pilag farm, and we couldn't just take him home. Mrs. Pilag said, "Go ahead, there are lots of cats here, and he won't be missed." Mintz rode home, squashed on my lap, and did not seem to mind that either.

Mintz settled into life with us and did not quarrel with Tippy or Spolite or anyone else. A picture of Mintz, Tippy, a rabbit and a chicken shows them all eating out of the same bowl. Mintz seemed to understand that rats in the corn-crib and mice in the chicken coop were fair game, and he would hunt them from time to time. He would bring partially eaten corpses and leave them on the front steps as proof of his diligence. But he was not terribly ambitious, so the rodents were in no danger of extinction.

Our parents had been warring with the rodents using traps in the house and elsewhere since we moved in. Momma refused to use poisons, and Papa did not dispute her stand. We had animals that might eat a poisoned rodent and thus could cause ourselves more harm than good. We hoped that Mintz would keep them at bay. Mintz seemed to do what he could, but he didn't work on weekends or if it was too hot or if the rats were really big. I remember a scene where some rats were spooked in the chicken coop and Mintz was there and the older brothers were encouraging him to go after them and he looked at the rats on the wall and at us and seemed to say, "Are you kidding?"

As the summer wound down, life changed again. The Briedis kids went home to Omaha. Jurit and Andrit went back to school at the one-room Star Prairie Elementary School. Root crops were harvested and stored. The grassy fields went to seed and milkweeds opened their pods and floated their future away on little downy parachutes. A fall scent was in the air and a feeling that colder times were coming. Although Tippy kept us company and Mintz got up from wherever he was napping and came out to say hello (he purred like a small engine), Max and I noticed how quiet it was around the yard during the day.

Several male turkeys had matured into very impressive dark-colored birds. Their feathers, iridescent in the sun, fascinated me—the colors would change from bronze to blue to green to black! They allowed me to pat their smooth broad backs, but they became aggressive toward the adults, and the boys had to be very careful. Momma thought that the boys teased them, but, in hindsight, I think they were being territorial and thought I should join their flock, so they were always nice to me.

Our lives revolved around the animals and the fields and napping and foraging. We did not have a television, and I don't recall anything on Jurit's radio other than music. My parents did not read newspapers or talk about world events when we were around. There was no mechanism to announce fighting in faraway places or weather disasters almost as they happen. No violent cartoons, movies or TV shows. The youngest children gave no thought to the fact that life held many unforeseen dangers.

Although it is more than 50 years ago as I tell this story, it is still hard to think about what happened that fall. One evening while waiting for supper, Andrit, Max, and I were chasing around the yard playing hide and seek. Tippy darted back and forth and barked occasionally; although he did not know the rules, he was always willing to play. Whoever was *it* encouraged Tippy to find the others. We got wound up and out of breath and kept running farther into the dark away from the yard light so that it would be harder for the *it* person to find us. Momma called us in to supper so we headed back. Behind us we heard a car braking hard on the gravel road and a thump and a yelp. We looked around and asked, "Where is Tippy?"

Feeling anxious, we went in to the kitchen. A moment later, there was a knock on the door. A stranger asked to talk to Papa who left and was gone for what seemed like a long time. Momma told us to sit down and start eating. But the yelping and whimpering in the driveway drew us all outside. Papa carried Tippy and laid him down gently under the yard light. Tippy did not try to lift his head or get up. His eyes were glassy and blood pooled from his mouth. Trembling spasms shook his body.

We stood around the dying dog in complete shock. I did not try to touch him and could not understand how our pal could look so strange. The yard light cast an eerie glow over everything as murmured questions passed to the stranger. Someone covered Tippy with an old coat. Andrit translated for us that Tippy had run out in front of the man's car and he could not brake in time. The driver offered to shoot Tippy to put him out of his misery. When the older boys heard that they started pleading with our parents. "No, no, please don't shoot him. Don't let him shoot Tippy. He will get better." Max and I howled in protest.

Momma herded and pulled us three into the house and blocked the kitchen door so we could not go outside again. We were desperate to know what was happening with Tippy, so we climbed up on a counter to look out the window. Momma was glued to the screen door while Andrit looked over her shoulder. Jurit stayed outside with Papa and the stranger. The sound of Tippy's whimpering seared into my memory, but before any decision was made about using the gun, he grew quiet. We watched as the stranger talked to Papa and then slowly walked away.

Max and I did not understand what that meant. We kept asking Momma what they were going to do with Tippy. Momma did not answer and just looked at us and then out to the yard. We could see Papa and Jurit standing near Tippy. Papa's shoulders slumped as he looked down at the small mound covered by an old coat. When they finally came in they looked very sad and told us that Tippy had died.

Although we sat down at the table no one could eat any supper. Max and I cried until we couldn't breathe and Momma put us to bed. Eventually exhaustion silenced the house.

The next morning Papa got up very early and buried Tippy; we were not told where. During the next days and weeks I noticed that my parents would get a sad and worried look on their faces whenever I brought him up. So I stopped talking about him. About that time, I realized that the weight of a small stone had settled over my heart. Tippy had climbed in and would make himself felt for a long time to come.

Max and I went outside every day as usual, and every day we felt the loss of our pal. The empty yard was hard to bear. Sometimes our parents would talk about him when they didn't know we were nearby. They talked about how few cars ever came down our road and what a misfortune it was that Tippy and a car met in such a way. They talked about how it would have been better if the small ones had not seen him dying, but what could Papa have done? He did not know that Tippy was going to die until he put him down under the yard light and even then it was hard to grasp. Then they said almost simultaneously, "Thank God one of the children didn't run into the road."

Although I did not appreciate it at the time, the stranger was another example of the kind hearts living in South Dakota. He did not drive away leaving Tippy to die where he fell and he did what he could to help the situation. Max and I talked about Tippy frequently, but nothing seemed to lift the pall from our world. The joy we had felt and the interest in our projects was gone.

One day we were out in the fields when Max picked up a stick. As he walked, he smacked the heads off milkweed plants releasing a cloud of seeds. We came across some weathered and partially rotted boards. He pried one up and we saw several small mice and some bigger ones. He told me that I should lift the board all the way up and he would kill the mice. I was about to do it when I realized that Momma had said rodents could be killed if they were doing damage to our house or crops. I started to argue that mice living under a board out in the field should not be bothered. While we discussed whether we had jurisdiction to kill them, the mouse family made a run for the tall grass and escaped.

On the walk home we felt even worse while thinking about what we had tried to do and were more bewildered. We knew that Tippy's death had changed our world forever, but did not know what to do with that knowledge.

October 1953

That fall seemed made of gray and brown earth and cloudy skies although one day stands out in brilliant hues. Mr. Christopherson let us hand pick some corn fields after he had gone over them with machinery. We got half of what we picked to feed our livestock and poultry for the winter. I was there willing to help but with a tendency to be distracted. While the bigger people and even Max threw cobs into the wagon, I gazed around at a sky too blue to believe. It was so clear and the air crisp and fresh. The stubble and corn cobs were golden and crunched underfoot. I kept looking at the juxtaposition of the blue and gold and felt inspired.

I picked up a cob and folded back the dried leaves and formed the head and wings and tail of a duck. The cob was the body. I set my duck under the wagon and went for more. Pretty soon I had a whole flock of ducks. Momma asked what I was doing and I told her and she said I could keep three, but the rest had to be added to the pile in the wagon. I carried what I thought was about three (what I could carry in one trip) back to the car and climbed in and got to know them while everyone else kept working.

My mother's birthday is in October. No one else could make her traditional birthday torte, so she made it herself. The cake batter had so many eggs in it that it was a golden yellow. Many layered, this special cake had preserves in some layers and custard filling in others—all covered with a rich butter frosting. Everyone had a piece—I looked around and saw that there was no chance to snag any more. All the plates were swept clean and the remainder of the cake was put away in the fridge. With the outdoor jobs easing up now that the garden was harvested, our parents had a little more time to relax, so we started lobbying for a story. My older brothers asked Momma to tell us about how life was when she was born.

It was a cold and rainy October in 1915 when I was born at my parents' farm in the Medni area of Latvia. Your Grandmother had been running the farm alone since your Grandfather had been drafted into the army and he was away at War. The First World War had started in 1914 and both the Russians and Germans wanted control of the Baltic States. Your Grandfather was a cook in the Russian Army and was always grateful that he did not have to shoot at anyone.

Mother had sent my oldest siblings—Arvids, who was nine, and Erna, who was five—to live with Grandfather Rutkis farther away from the front lines. Six-year-old Albert and two-and-a-half-year-old Marta were home with her. Earlier that year, my Grandmother had died suddenly so the months before my birth had been sad and lonely. Mother was depressed, but there was still much hard work that she had to do. Crops had to be harvested and animals fed. Your Kalnin Grandparents lived in part of a large stone building that had once been an Inn and Tavern but was not used in that way any more. Tenants lived in some of the rooms and did work around the farm.

All the stress in my mother's life might have caused me to be born prematurely. I don't know but I do know that when I was born my mother said I was very thin and that my skin was so transparent that I looked blue. The midwife said, "This poor child is not long for this world so have her baptized as soon as possible."

A day or two later, my mother bundled up and put me inside her clothes against her chest because it was the warmest place she had and set off. She left Albert and Marta with a tenant and a relative, Olga Purvis, (I was named after this relative) drove the wagon. A cold drizzle and a lowering sky set the mood. The wheels creaked and rattled and my mother had to brace herself with one arm while holding me in place with the other. She was very weary, but determined that her baby would be baptized. The roads were muddy and rutted and the going was slow. The horse strained in the traces and sometimes stumbled. Since there were no phones she did not even know if the minister would be there when they arrived.

Fortunately the minister was home and invited them in. He performed the baptism ceremony and blessed the baby and everyone else present. Then he said, "Do not fear, mother, it is not the flesh that keeps a person alive but the spirit. This child has a very strong spirit. So take little Olga home and don't worry."

When Momma finished the story Papa said, "And she still has a strong spirit." I tried to imagine Momma being small and thin. I was completely dependent on her for all the important things of life and saw her as never tiring and always available so thoughts about her being vulnerable made me uneasy. I asked some questions about the horse instead. Momma said the horse's name was Milda and that she had been a present from Grandmother's parents when she married our Grandfather Andrejs Kalnins.

As the days grew chilly, we spent less time outside. Even Zimala came in at night, and Spolite made a bigger nest for herself. The poultry, outside for shorter periods, sat in the sun but always roosted early. Life was a quiet routine again. Wood fed the furnace in the living room which kept the house toasty. By the time I got up in the morning, a fire was going either there or in the kitchen; I was always warm. Over the years I have learned that you really can't enjoy breakfast unless you are nice and warm while eating it.

Just before Thanksgiving our parents made plans that Papa and the two older brothers would visit the Briedis family over the long Thanksgiving weekend. They were going to deliver some root crops and have a look at Omaha. Momma had to stay home because someone had to take care of the animals and although I was always willing to help she said I was too small to do it by myself.

Once the travelers were sent off, Max and I found some indoor activities but did not stray far from the kitchen. Momma was making another torte because Papa's birthday would fall right after the weekend and she wanted it to be ready when he got home. Tortes always meant spoons to be licked and frosting that needed sampling.

She told me much later that she was uneasy that weekend because she couldn't remember a time without other adults nearby. In Germany in the DP camps there were always many people around. Since she grew up in a large family, she was used to company. Our farm was far from any neighbor so she noticed the isolation.

She started thinking about her mother with whom she could not communicate directly but at least by then she got word about her through Erna. Ernina (Ernnnina—there is no symbol in the English language to denote the long n sound in her name) could write to the family in the homeland because the Communists were not quarreling with Canada, thus mail passed freely between Latvia and Canada. Ernina would forward information to my mother about the family left behind.

Momma's thoughts often wandered back to her childhood at home on the farm. She told me years later that thoughts about childhood are a path that never disappears and once you start on it you can get lost for hours.

As she thought about being alone with small children Momma remembered a story that her mother, Mimite (Berta Kalnins), told her.

> *It was maybe 1916 or 1917 and the War continued to grind on. You were a tiny child. Your father was still away. We had only one horse—others in the neighborhood had been confiscated for the War effort and were never seen again. Milda did everything—pulled the plow for the garden, the wagon for trips to town or to gather crops or hay from the fields. Without her, it would be very hard to feed the family.*
>
> *One day some officials arrived in a wagon of their own and came in to the house and asked for Berta Kalnins. They said they were sorry but they had to have Milda for the war effort and that they were sure that I would understand and*

cooperate. I argued against it saying that the horse was needed for farm work. "My husband is away and I have to do so much work by myself that I can't cope without the horse." But the officials wouldn't listen and were getting restless. They wanted the horse so they could be on their way.

My arguments and pleadings were not being heard so I looked at them long and hard. My heart in my throat and hands shaking I said "Fine, I will give you the horse but you have to do one thing for me." They murmured their ascent that they would do whatever they could, etc. By this point you three small ones were clinging to my dress and hiding behind me. I told them, "Before you go, take these children down to the creek and drown them."

The men were shocked and said. "Well, if you need the horse that much we won't take it" and left in a hurry. They slammed the door so hard on the way out that plaster fell from the ceiling. Milda stayed on the farm and with her help enough food was harvested for the family. Later when your father heard about the incident he said that if he survived the War he would let Milda live out her life on the farm.

Momma thought about her mother's courage in the face of very difficult circumstances and assured herself that she would be okay until Papa came home.

When Papa and the big brothers arrived they were all in a good mood and had stories about their visit. Papa said that the biggest surprise was that Mrs. Briedis had made a birthday cake for him. Momma wondered, "But how did she know?" Papa said, "I wondered too and asked her and she said that when we sent those sponsorship papers our birth dates were included." Momma said, "After supper you can have more cake because I made one too." Papa beamed and was very happy to hear that news.

Papa brought colorful jackets for all of us that were sent by the Briedis family as thanks for looking after all the kids for the summer. He said he enjoyed the drive and was no longer nervous about driving on the highway or in a big city. After everyone had some of Papa's birthday torte, Jurit went upstairs. He had gotten an electric train set the previous Christmas and now he set it up in the boys' large attic bedroom. We all spent hours watching the train and watching Jurit add on more tracks to make the route longer and more interesting.

Parsla

I don't remember the rest of that year or how we celebrated that Christmas probably because there was a startling event on January 2nd of 1954. Papa went out to the barn on that weekend morning and ran back calling to Momma that a calf had arrived, Zimala had had her calf. We all threw on some clothes and rushed out to the barn. A spindly legged and still wet calf wobbled around Zimala's stall.

The baby was shivering intensely. Andrits went back to the house and got an old coat to cover her and Zimala kept licking the baby calf's head with such energy that she almost knocked her over. The adults cooed about how cute she was and wondered where she should stay—should it be with Zimala or in her own pen? Had she eaten yet? I made eye contact with the small bovine and as I looked into her dark beady eyes, I sensed I had at last met a worthy adversary.

She was all black but for a tiny white spot on her forehead and a bit of white on one front and one hind ankle. We named her Parsla which means *flake* in Latvian—*sniega parsla* is a snow flake. The parents always called her Parsla but later we kids nicknamed her Tubby. Like all our cows she probably thought her name was *maja, maja* which was what they responded to because it meant *come home and you will get a snack.*

The next few days were very busy. Momma taught little Parsla to drink her milk from a pail because if she was allowed to nurse too long she could not be let out in the pasture with Zimala when she got older. It was also important that she get plenty of the first milk—the colostrum—with all the important stuff in it.

Momma did not know anything about antibodies just that her mother had always said it was important for calves to get that milk from their mothers. But Parsla could not drink all the milk Zimala produced so soon there was sweet milk and all the other products that we had learned to enjoy.

I wanted to feed her but after one attempt where she sucked my fingers into her mouth and I could barely get my hand free I let Momma manage the feeding event. As gentle and compliant as Zimala was Parsla was the opposite—willful and stubborn. Momma had to be careful when she brought the pail in to Parsla's pen because she would smash it so hard with her little square head that she ended up spilling some. Parsla wanted her milk and she wanted it now!

Momma said I was very careful about making sure her pen was well bedded with fresh straw and that I would try to brush her with Zimala's brush. Momma did not know that I was studying Parsla. Learning to scrutinize the adversary came in handy many years later when I had a career where such knowledge was useful. I soon knew that it was best not to turn my back on her because she would charge and butt me with her head and send me flying. As I picked myself up from the straw she bounced away and I was sure there was a smirk on her face.

We had to teach her to be tied up and to be willing to be led. She resisted vigorously and would throw herself back against the rope so that you thought she was going to pull her head off. But eventually she gave in. Trying to get a halter on her was never easy; Momma would give her a treat and she would gobble that up and still toss her head and dodge and try to escape.

In South Dakota spring arrived early and by March the snow was gone and the scent of big changes was in the air. Momma and Papa always worked at keeping the yard tidy. At that time of year our yard was muddy from the melting snow so some boards were laid down where we could walk and leave most of the dirt outside. One day Momma and I were out in the yard and she told me what she planned to do. We needed to drain the yard and we would do that by opening little ditches between the ruts left by the car and connect those to other pools and ruts. The plan was to get the water to head downhill and out of our yard.

We spent a morning on our project—Momma had a shovel and I had a small stick. If I couldn't move enough dirt I would tell Momma and she would bring in her heavy machinery. The light danced on the little rivulets of water and I had to concentrate on the task at hand rather than wander off in a daydream about how the little rivers passed by tiny towns with tiny people living in them. By the end of the morning most of the standing water had left the yard. The memory of that day and the pleasure of learning something new were never forgotten.

As a child I did not realize that gathering fresh food from the garden to make all meals from scratch was a lot of work. Main meals were made up of various forms of hamburger either as meat loaf, casseroles, or meat patties, usually flavored with onions and sometimes celery. We used our own potatoes until we ran out toward spring. We ate various root crops and cabbages also. In the winter Momma would make a roasting pan filled with sauerkraut; and sometimes she would roast chicken or turkey pieces along with the sauerkraut.

She made all kinds of soups including a meatball soup that was Jurit's favorite. She liked to make soups because she could save some in the fridge and then warm it up when the hungry tribe came home looking as if they might eat the furniture.

I was most interested in the desserts, which were of interest to Papa as well, so Momma usually had something on hand. One favorite she made from whipped cream of wheat, cooked and flavored with the juice of cranberries or other berries—whatever was available. She then whipped it to a light and very fluffy consistency. Just before serving, she floated it on a light fruit sauce. Fresh fruits, cooked and strained, were always best when thickened with corn starch and sugar. The combination of flavors was heavenly.

Momma made lots of apple pies and various forms of *plats maizes*. Usually, once a weekend in the winter, she made pancakes—with and without yeast. Potato pancakes were well received, but the favorite were crepes made with lots of eggs and fried very thin. Papa usually cooked those pancakes himself after Momma had mixed up the batter.

One day as he was frying the pancakes and we were eating them faster than he could cook them, he told us this story.

I had no brothers or sisters. When I was three, my mother died and I went to live with my mother's parents and my aunts and uncles. When I was four, the First World War started and the Russians and Germans struggled for control of Latvia. Many Latvians fled east to avoid the fighting. A Russian owned the factory where my uncles worked. When the owner decided to pack it up and move the factory back to Russia to preserve his investment, he offered to take his workers along. Not knowing what else they would do once the factory left, my relatives all evacuated east into Russia.

My father had been drafted into the Russian Army and went away to the front lines. When my father came to visit me, he brought me numerous books. He told me to read them and to study hard in school and to remember that "what you have up here (tapping his forehead) is not easily taken away from you. Study hard so that you don't have to be a laborer like I have been." The last time I saw him I was about six which would have been in late 1916 or 1917. I heard that he had died in the war, but then I also heard from another source that he moved to Estonia and remarried, but I never knew for sure.

I started school in Russia and became fluent in the Russian language. I always did well in school and languages came easily to me. We lived in a medium-sized city in an apartment building owned by a Russian couple. When they learned that I was an orphan, the lady of that house became friendly and invited me over. She gave me treats and would make pancakes for me. She fried them very thin in butter and drizzled them with honey. They just melted in my mouth. I guess my life-long love of pancakes began with those wonderful crepes of my childhood.

Life seemed quite fine to me. My Grandmother doted on me and now the landlady seemed willing to do the same. Things changed when I came home from school one afternoon and heard my Grandmother arguing with my uncles. As I listened in the hallway, I gleaned that the Russian couple wanted to adopt me because they had no children of their own.

My uncles thought it was a good idea. They argued that these folks had money and property and would be able to send me to school; what could my family offer me? Grandmother Anna was completely against the idea. I ran into the room, hugged her, and cried that I did not want to live with anyone but them. They dropped the discussion, but I always felt insecure and was deeply hurt when from time to time my uncles would tease me and say they were going to leave me behind in Russia. I never went to the landlady's apartment again, and once she learned that there would be no adoption, she stopped asking me.

It was a good thing that I did not stay in Russia and returned with my relatives to Latvia in 1920 when I was ten years old. Many Russian property owners were sent to Siberia when the Communists took over; if I had stayed, I might have had that same fate.

When he was done with his story, we had eaten as many pancakes as we could hold and Papa could finally sit down and eat a plate of his own.

Aunt Erna Visits

Jurit worked whenever he could during our first summer on the Christopherson farm. The following spring, farm work in our area picked up again, so he was happy to help the Scholtens and the Christophersons and anyone else who would hire him. He saved every dime because he hoped to buy a car as soon as he turned fifteen and could get a driver's license. A few weeks before Jurit's birthday in early June, Papa heard about a good deal on a 1936 Ford which he could have for $125. Although Jurit did not have that much money, the parents thought he should get it anyway so they made up the difference. One evening we all went to get the car and bring it home.

Jurit had been driving tractors since the previous summer, so it was no problem for him to drive a standard shift vehicle. The parents commented on how confident he was and how easily he maneuvered his little Ford. We followed him home over back roads because he did not yet have a license. When we got back to the farm, we all piled in and he took us for a little drive on the country roads. He was thrilled and could not stop smiling. Two cars in the family were much more convenient. Jurit could take us to the store or to the movies or to the swimming pool on really hot days. He could also get jobs that were beyond walking distance.

Around that time, we got a letter from Ernina that she had gotten all the proper paperwork and that she would be arriving for a visit on August 1st. At last a relative was going to make an appearance! Momma was very pleased and smiled more frequently. The whole family was excited. I asked Momma whether Aunt Erna knew how to bake a cake. She said that her sister was a good cook and could make all sorts of things. Then I asked Momma if Ernina liked horses. Momma said she wasn't sure but I would have a chance to ask her when she arrived.

The Briedis boys had also arrived to spend part of the summer with us. When he wasn't reading Andrit ran around with Uldis and Janis. Sometimes Janis played with us, but most of the time he preferred the bigger boy activities. Max and I were always together so that when Momma called us she always used both our names. Max liked to chat and I became a lazy talker. Max would inform the world what I wanted to eat, what I didn't want to eat, and what I thought about this or that. When I started a sentence, he would complete it. He had become my spokesperson, and I was content to let him communicate with the world of real people. I often drifted off into a fantasy world with lots of horses in it and many adventures for me. I did find that a bit of cake made the fantasies more vivid and Max could often be talked into fetching some for me.

It was before Ernina's visit that Jurit hurt his hand in the barbed wire fencing accident and the same time that the bees were aggravated by having pee poured on their heads. But all those problems had been resolved by late July when Momma started counting the days until Ernina would arrive. Now that Jurit had his license, he was the one who would drive to Sioux City to pick her up. He decided to spruce up his automobile by painting the rear fenders and the spare tire cover silver—the rest of the car was a dull black.

He got the paint and some brushes and he and Andrit set to work. Max and I wanted to help, but Jurit said we could not do the precise brush strokes that were needed. We were outraged that he considered us inept and marched inside complaining to Momma. She tried to mollify us, but since there was no cake on hand she was having little success. At that moment Mr. Christopherson drove into the yard.

We trotted out to meet him. He often brought something for us including an occasional chocolate bar. This time he lifted out a large cardboard box from his trunk that was thumping and trying to burst open. As soon as he pulled the rope loose, a puppy came tumbling out. Puppy ducked his head and wagged his whole body and ran around asking to be petted by all of us. He was older than Tippy had been when he arrived and his fur was longer, but he was the same tawny color. He had a white chest and paws and a soft silky coat. He was doing his best to charm us and after a moment or two he proved to be irresistible. When we talked about what we should call him, Momma suggested *Duksis* (Dukseet for every day use) because one of her childhood dogs had that name. We all agreed that Duksis would be a good name.

Mr. Christopherson smiled as he watched us tumbling around. Momma said later that he had noticed the previous fall how sad we were after Tippy died and had decided then to find a new puppy for us. Max and I were occupied with our new pal and completely forgot about painting Jurit's car. We played with Duksit for the rest of the day, but always well away from the road.

Every morning I went outside to look around for Duksit, reassured when he would appear with a grin on his face and his tail waving. He quickly learned who was who in the farmyard and did not quarrel with anyone. He also learned the sound of Papa's or Jurit's car and would run around the yard to clear all the poultry and any stray rabbits. He would wait by the garage while the car was parked and then accompany the driver to the porch steps. He had given himself a job.

The day finally arrived and late in the afternoon Jurit left for Sioux City. Andrit remembered having met Ernina in Germany, but Max did not. I had never seen any relatives. Jurit was the only one who had met Momma's parents and siblings in Latvia before the war. He still remembered walking down the streets of Riga on the way to Aunt Austra's apartment when candles and lights decorated the city for the holidays. Our sister Laura was just a toddler, but she felt the excitement too. Everyone celebrated Christmas with songs and cake and all together in a cheery group. I knew nothing about large gatherings of relatives and was very curious about Aunt Erna.

We small ones went to bed before they arrived. The next morning we heard a strange voice that bubbled with laughter talking to Momma in the kitchen. Andrits was up too and quickly herded us upstairs under one of the beds. He convinced us that we should hide there. We had hidden there before, but personally I did not want to do it that morning, but my decision-making is not the best when I am barely awake. The parents and Ernina searched the yard and called for us when they noticed our absence. Jurit finally found us. As soon as he did, Max and I crawled out, but Andrit wouldn't come out to meet Ernina. Papa leaned down and said to him, "If you don't come out, someone else will eat your share of the pancakes."

Very soon Andrit joined the rest of us in the kitchen to meet our Aunt. She hugged and kissed us and picked me up. Her lap was soft and she was fragrant with perfume and quick to laugh. Momma and Papa were both beaming—they had already been talking for hours. Words still rushed out because they had not seen each other for five years. I had never seen my mother so joyously happy.

After breakfast Jurit took all the rest of the kids to town while I took Ernina by the hand and led her on a tour of the farm. I showed her all the poultry and Spolite. Mintz and Duksits introduced themselves. Then I tried to take her to Zimala, but she was across the creek with Parsla and the rest of the cattle. Ernina had city shoes on and could not wade across. It was also very hot. By the time I brought her back to the house she was tired and needed to rest in the shade. During our walk I talked to her about horses and tried to determine where she stood on the equine question.

The adults settled in the shade in some lawn chairs and Duksit and I sat on the grass. Ernina said that her trip had been fine and it was interesting to look out the window of the train and see all the towns and farms and cities along the way—it had been a two-day trip from Montreal. When she got off the train at

Sioux City, she looked around for Jurit (Momma had written and told her that he would be picking her up). "All of a sudden a tall tanned young man came up to me and addressed me in Latvian. I was so surprised. I was looking for the boy I last saw in Germany and did not imagine the young man he has become."

Then my parents asked what had happened when she tried to sneak across the border to visit us. She had an expressive face and made large eyes as she launched into her story. She had a friend Voldemars who had come to Canada after the War from Czechoslovakia and he also had relatives in America. He was desperate to visit them, she said, but he wanted a companion for a trip across the border. He told her that he had studied some maps and knew where they would need to get off the train. It would be a short walk through some woods and he felt sure they could do it. She said she had misgivings, but so very much wanted to see us. It had been so long since she had seen any family.

> So I packed some things in a small suitcase and we took the train and got off where Voldemars said we should and then we walked into the woods, but it got dark. We did not want to risk getting lost so we sat down and slept fitfully until daybreak. Then we walked some more and when we came out of the woods, crossed a road (Voldemars had a compass and we just kept walking south) and walked a little farther and there was a farm.
>
> The mailbox had an American flag on it. Voldemars was smiling and I felt great relief because it had been so easy. All of a sudden two black sedans pulled up, blocking us against the side of the road. Uniformed men got out and motioned for us to get into the back seat—me in one car and Voldemar in the other!
>
> We were taken to a jail. Since I couldn't speak any English, I did not know what would happen next. To pass the time I started to draw some flowers on a napkin and then the next thing I knew a woman was pushing some paper and colored pencils across the table and motioning that I should draw a color picture. So I did and you know all I like to draw is flowers. I spent the next several weeks drawing flowers from morning to night. They also gave me crayons and more paper and even the guards had me do some pictures. It made the time pass very quickly. Finally, they sent me back to Canada.
>
> When I got back to Montreal I met up with Voldemasr and he said that he played cards and got some extra food out of it. We agreed that we would not try that again and would have to get the necessary documents in order to cross the border legally.

Their voices moved off to discussions about world events and old friends and other relatives and I think I dozed off. Soon everyone else came home and it was time to make supper. Ernina and Momma talked in the kitchen and in the garden and on the way to the garden and on the way to milk Zimala and all around the yard as Momma did her daily duties. I liked it that Momma was so cheery—she didn't even notice when I opened the fridge to see what treats I might find there.

Ernina pitched right in and helped with all the work that needed to be done. One of the things she offered to do was milk the cow. I agreed to go along and make sure that Zimala did not give her any trouble. I told Zimala that Ernina was our aunt and was visiting from far away.

Zimala gave Ernina a good sniff but once she spoke to her in Latvian, Zimala relaxed, her ears drooped down, and she burped up a cud. Zimala stood as if she were tied to a post (as she always did) and chewed diligently. Ernina was impressed with my ability to control the cow.

Although Parsla was now an adolescent, she still eyed the milk pail with interest—just in case there was anything for her. Momma would give her a pail of whey with warm water added to it from time to time even though she had been weaned. I warned Ernina to watch out for her because she liked to give people a strong push with her head. She also tried to give my face a rough wash with her tongue. After we were done with the milking, Zimala and Parsla wandered off to the brush growing near the creek. They joined the beef herd and spent a good part of the day hiding from the heat and the flies.

It was very warm in August in South Dakota and the little creek was barely a trickle so Jurit took the boys to the pool quite frequently. I would not go unless Momma came too. One day Ernina said she would like to go along, but she did not have a swimming suit. The parents took her to the store and got one for her. Then we all went to the pool. Ernina had not been swimming for a long time and was quite pale, so we went home early to avoid the risk of sunburn. Jurit and all the boys stayed longer.

On another occasion, Papa and Ernina were in town when they ran in to Mrs. Smith at the grocery store. Mrs. Smith invited all of us to her place for Sunday lunch. Papa told her that Ernina was visiting" us and we also had the Briedis boys. She said, "It is no problem—bring them all." When they got home, they told Momma and she said, "We have to bake a torte. In fact, we have to bake two so that we have one at home as well." I nodded my head in approval.

When Sunday arrived, we piled into both cars and made the short trip to the Smith farm. Lunch was pleasant with lots of good food and the easy sound of the adults talking. The small boys prodded one another and made faces trying to make each other laugh. I was right next to Max so I reminded him that Momma would want him to behave better. He looked stricken and then looked at Momma. Since she was not paying attention, he was drawn back into the small-boy behavior. Finally, lunch was over and we all went outside to look around the farm. As usual, my main interest was to see what the Smiths had in their barn.

Since it was summer, most of the livestock was outside in the pasture, but they did have some pigs in a shed. One of the pigs had a litter of piglets. The little ones were running around and squealing and jumping over each other. I was fascinated with their antics. I asked Momma why Spolite did not have any children. Momma was startled and finally said that she probably will have children. Later that fall Mr. Smith came with a trailer and took Spolite away for a few days and then brought her back. My parents were vague about the purpose of that trip.

One of the chores Ernina volunteered to do was go to the mailbox to check for mail. Our mailbox was not at the end of our driveway but at a crossroads some distance away. Momma wrote to people she met in Germany and a cousin who was now in Connecticut and the Briedis family and various other Latvian friends. She always brightened when there was a letter for her.

I offered to accompany Ernina and discussed horses with her on the walk. She came up with the idea that I should be an imaginary horse and she would be the driver. She tied a shawl around my waist and suspended a small cardboard box between "the reins" behind me. She held the ends of the shawl and I led the way. We put the mail in the box and then we came home again. As I got used to the game, I started frisking and pulling harder until Ernina pleaded with her "little horse" to take it easy and not run so fast.

The small circle of Latvians that my parents knew was shrinking. The Briedis family had moved to Omaha, Gunars went to a larger city in search of a better job, and Sophie and Fritz Eversons moved to Racine, Wisconsin. They had all come to America before we did and wanted better opportunities.

On one of our trips to the mailbox, we picked up a letter from the Eversons. They wrote about life in general and then told a story about buying a car. They had saved every dime and when they had enough went to a car dealer and picked out a very nice new Oldsmobile. They made the deal and paid in cash. A short time after driving it home, a policeman came to their door and started asking them questions about where they had gotten all that cash to buy the car. He was not satisfied until they brought out their bank book and showed the deposits, large and small, that they had all made over the last year. The officer looked over the pages and then he quietly closed the book and handed it back to them. Then he went away.

When Papa came home Momma told him about the Eversons experience with purchasing the car and Papa said that he hoped we wouldn't do anything to attract the attention of the police.

Before the month was over, Papa told us that his boss's wife wanted us to come over for a visit one afternoon because she wanted to meet Ernina. They had been involved in the attempt to get Ernina out of jail that first summer when she entered the country illegally. Mr. Shaw had written a letter to the authorities in New York. Soon thereafter we got dressed up (for Max and me that meant we had to wear shoes) and then we all piled into Jurit's car and drove into Vermillion.

The Shaws lived in a large house with a manicured lawn. We all went out into the back yard and sat on lawn chairs under large shade trees. Cookies and lemonade appeared and disappeared almost as fast. They had a pond in their backyard and so we went over to see if it had any fish in it and when none were visible, we started playing with the water. I don't know what the rest of the boys did for the afternoon, but Max and I were completely entertained by the ripples we could make in the pool.

The ladies talked for a couple hours although it was not easy going since Momma and Ernina did not know much English and Mrs. Shaw did not know Latvian. Momma said that Mrs. Shaw was sad that her son had chosen to go to a military college rather than pursue the violin which was her preference. She loved music and was very disappointed that he had chosen what she viewed as a brutal occupation. Momma said to Ernina later that she felt Mrs. Shaw wanted to "get things off her heart" and that it didn't matter that they could not contribute much to the conversation.

At the end of August, the Briedis parents drove up from Omaha to pick up their boys and to stay for a long weekend. It might have been Labor Day weekend. School was going to start soon everywhere and this year Max, who turned six in September, would have to go too. But first there was a long lazy end-of-the-summer get-together with the adults visiting about things that interested them and this time Ernina was there too.

On a hot afternoon the conversation turned to how Ernina got out of Latvia in the fall of 1944. She settled into her lawn chair and started her story.

> *It was a terrible time, as you know, because you left around that time too. I left a little later from Liepaja. My plan was to leave by boat and travel to Germany, so I registered with the many other refugees who were trying to do the same. I was given a ticket for a specific day and was told to appear at the dock early in the morning.*
>
> *In the meantime, I stayed in the cellar of a bombed building with the few possessions I could carry and a little food. It was cold and dark in that cellar and all the people there were anxious about the future. We heard terrible things about the Russians and just wanted to get away before they got there.*

On the day of the departure I wrapped my things into a shawl and started to walk to the dock. I was hurrying because I did not want to miss my chance to get on that boat. All of a sudden I heard the jangle of something hitting the pavement. I stopped and scooped my alarm clock up and thrust it back into my makeshift bag. A few more steps and it fell out again. I was feeling exasperated but picked it up and pushed it deeper into my bag. I was almost running now because it was a long walk to the dock and I could not afford any delay.

I walked fast for some minutes when I heard the jangle and jingle and thud of the fallen alarm. Now I was truly exasperated, but I did not want to leave the clock because it was a gift from my Grandfather Rutkis. He gave it to me when I lived with them during the First War when our father was away and our mother sent Arvids and me to live with them. It always reminded me how kind and patient he was.

I looked around in desperation and spotted it, but this time it had rolled under a chain link fence. There was no gate within sight and I knew that I was now dangerously late for my boat trip. But I looked around some more and saw a stick and tried to work the clock closer to the fence so that I could grab it but every few inches it would fall the other way and I would have to struggle to get it moving in my direction. I don't know how long it took, but I finally got it to where I could reach it. I decided to hold it in my hand and carry it the rest of the way.

Beads of sweat dotted my forehead and I was hot and out of breath when I arrived at the dock. I presented my ticket and the attendant looked it over and said, "You are too late. Your place was taken by someone else." I was shocked and exclaimed bitterly, "But I have a reservation!" He would not budge and said, "There is no more room. All I can do is write you in for tomorrow's boat—there is no room on this one."

As I walked away, I had the urge to throw the clock into the harbor. As I put my arm back to pitch it a security guard grabbed me and said it is forbidden to throw anything into the water. Angry and embarrassed, I put it in my pocket. It was a long walk back to that cellar and another long night. The next morning I left even earlier to make sure that I would be there on time. This morning the clock behaved and stayed where I put it. When I got to the dock I noticed objects floating in the water and looking closer I realized that there were suitcases and clothes and shoes and then all of a sudden I grasped that there were bodies floating too.

I went to the dock office where other people were gathered and was told that the ship that I had hoped to take the previous day was torpedoed some distance out in the Baltic and that it sank. Everyone on board had died. I couldn't absorb what I heard and my knees started to collapse. I made it to a low wall and sat down.

The clock had delayed me enough to keep me off that boat. God used an ordinary thing, but something I valued, to stop me from meeting the fate of all those other people. My Grandfather's gift and God's will saved me. It is beat up from the falls and the glass is gone, but it still keeps good time and wakes me in the mornings. I think about those events every time I see it.

Everyone sat quietly and thought about her story. They agreed that it had been a miracle that kept her away from that ship. "So how did you finally get to Germany?" Mrs. Briedis asked. "I took a train a few days later and got there with no further problems," Ernina replied.

As I tagged along with them while they did various chores that evening, I thought about Ernina's story, but it was too hard to think that I might never have met her. So I pushed those thoughts away and asked her whether she had any horse stories from her childhood.

Max started school that fall and had to get up early to walk there with Andrit. Jurit drove into town to go to the Vermillion High School and I think sometimes he dropped off his brothers at school as well. Max did not like getting up so early and complained that he hated school and hoped it would burn down. I remember Max coming home and speaking gibberish with Andrit (he was learning English). The next thing I knew, I understood what they were talking about; the English language was no longer a mystery. That transition was seamless for me, but the loss of Max as a daily companion was another matter.

Momma and Ernina were busy all day chatting and doing chores. Ernina was willing to help with whatever the task was so Momma's load was lightened. Ernina was very willing to burst into laughter at any good story. The sisters kept each other amused all day long. I did not want to stay indoors so I went out and got a walking stick and called Duksit and we went for a march around the property. One day I came upon Zimala and Parsla lying down back to back in the fall sun and chewing their cuds. I felt drowsy so I crawled in between them and lay down.

It was a warm and comfy spot and I didn't wake up until they got up to go back to grazing. I hung around with them for the rest of the morning and imagined myself to be part of their herd. I found a couple longer sticks that I used as my "front legs" so I could walk around with them while the cows worked at getting grass into their bellies.

Momma said that for the rest of that fall whenever weather permitted I would go out and spend part of the day with the cows. They were very tolerant and never minded me crawling over them or around them or just sitting and leaning against them when they took their rest. Parsla and I reached a truce of sorts and she stopped trying to push me around. I learned their body language and could tell their mood—when they were going to lie down or get up or move out.

I noticed how Parsla would sidle up to Zimala and push at her with her head. Zimala would stop chewing her cud and start washing Parsla from behind her ears all the way up her neck. Zimala's rough tongue was heaven for her offspring. Parsla's head would droop lower and lower until her muzzle was resting on the ground. After many minutes Zimala would decide that the job was done, but Parsla would not relent and would push Zimala's neck until her mother gave in.

When they were in the barn, I took their brush and started working on the same areas for both of them. They stood so still that they could have been statutes. I made a note of the effect that the brushing had on them and also found that it was a soothing activity for me. Momma said years later that I spoke cow language because they listened to me when I wanted them to do something.

On a fine fall day, when Ernina and I were outside, I dragged out a hammer and some nails from the tool shed. Then I found some small boards and blocks of wood in the kindling pile. I brought everything to the steps and sat down and studied my materials. Ernina asked immediately what I wanted to make. I told her a cow.

She suggested things I could do, but let me do all the hammering and did not try to take over the project. I nailed four legs to a scrap of two-by-four that had a diagonally cut end. The legs were more or less the same length, so when I was finished, it could stand on all fours. Only a four-year-old and an indulgent aunt could tell that it was a cow.

She then found some smaller pieces and suggested I nail them together to form the neck and the head and a couple ears. She told me if I didn't pound the nails in too hard all the pieces could move so I could change the position from head down grazing to head up looking around. She also got a piece of twine and suggested that I nail that on the back as a tail. My cow was looking better and better. After I was satisfied that the job was done, I started thinking about building bigger cows. Then it occurred to me that I could build horses as well. In the next month I built several of each. I would carry my "herd" around and set it up in new grazing areas, but they were rather cumbersome. Once they were set up either grazing or looking around, there wasn't much more that I could do with them.

Although I liked my creations better than the corncob ducks of the previous fall (they were attacked by rodents and chickens and I think Spolite polished them off), I was still not satisfied. Even I could tell they had no relationship to the beautiful Palimino horses I saw at the parade. But for now they would have to do.

When the brothers came home from school Max showed me his workbooks and his assignments. He described the games they played at recess. He seemed to be more enthusiastic about recess than the classroom work. Since we now did not spend almost every waking moment together, things were changing for us. He was developing other interests while I was spending even more time in a fantasy world of my own making.

We didn't play outside after dark, and we understood that Duksit should always be discouraged from going close to the road. The evenings were quiet with the boys doing homework and Momma and Ernina doing dishes and visiting. Papa would join in too. I thought that having a relative visit was a very fine thing and hoped that more of them would appear.

Instead, one morning Momma announced that in a few days Ernina would be leaving. Her three-month permit was going to be up and she would have to return to Canada. I was dismayed, but somewhat appeased when she said she would come again next year. Momma was very sad; that sadness lasted well after Ernina was gone.

I thought about how things might have been if we still lived in the homeland among the relatives. I understood that it was very far away and that we couldn't go there but that we might some day. I decided we would take Mintz and Duksit with us, but wondered how we would move the cows. Although I had more time to think about such things, my attention span was short.

Winter on the Horizon

Every day after my outdoor expeditions, I checked in at the kitchen to see what was happening there. Momma baked almost all the bread we ate: a whole wheat version or a Latvian sourdough rye which has a very special flavor. On some occasion, Momma, had offered a piece to Mrs. Shaw and she became addicted to it. She even drove out to the country to pick it up. She dropped in on us and had some coffee and chatted and chatted. Momma nodded, but I doubt that she understood much of what Mrs. Shaw was saying. Mrs. Shaw had a big smile when Momma handed her a couple loaves. The bread was good and sometimes I had a piece of that bread and then followed it up with a piece of cake.

There was snow on the ground as Duksit and I wandered down to the creek on a day when everyone was in school and Papa was at work. The cows were in the barn and Momma was working in the house. Mr. Christopherson had moved his herd back to his place so the fields were quiet and empty. I looked for abandoned birds' nests. They were much easier to spot when all the leaves were gone. Sometimes they contained real treasures—eggs that had not hatched. When I found one, I carried it home right away, cradled carefully in my mitten.

But that day the nests I found were empty. I kept walking when I noticed a gnarled, almost black, piece of a branch. The trees by the creek dropped their branches from time to time. They lost their bark but the wood remained hard and shiny in various hues. The way the branch curved and the size interested me. I picked it up and realized that it could easily be a horse's head and neck.

I carried it on the rest of my walk and took it home. I tucked it away behind the chicken coop and took it out for my jaunts around the farm. It was light enough to carry easily and my imagination filled in a beautiful black horse that I was riding all around the acreage. Before the snow got too deep, I found a couple more specimens and added them to my collection. The next spring and summer I found even more. I attached binder twine for reins and would rotate which one I was "riding" on any given day.

One Latvian family that stayed in the area was the Mellups. He worked as a janitor at the University, although he had had a much more interesting job in the homeland. Middle-aged, they had decided not to move to a bigger city and bought a small house in Vermillion. They had no children and Mrs. Mellups always brought little toys and treats for Max and me. We liked going to their home to visit because she doted on us. It was at their house that I remember seeing a television for the first time.

One evening when we were there *Lassie* was on and we watched it with total attention. A crisis occurred when puppies fell into a hole and Lassie had to get the attention of humans so that they could be rescued. When I got very upset over the plight of the puppies, the bigger brothers got exasperated that I couldn't grasp that it wasn't real. It bothered me for a long time and although I wanted to believe that everything turned out all right, I just wasn't sure.

I don't remember that Christmas, but I am sure that we got some toys or picture books or maybe something useful. The one thing I wanted was a pony, but whenever I asked her about it, Momma said I was not old enough to handle one. I wasn't interested in pressuring her since I had learned how rambunctious Parsla could be. If a pony was stronger and faster, then I could be in trouble. I agreed to wait a while.

It had gotten cold and with snow on the ground, I didn't spend as much time outside. But Momma said I never complained about having nothing to do. I could entertain myself for hours with simple things. Some part of every day I spent feeding and bedding the animals and the poultry. Sometimes Mintz would be curled up and asleep on Zimala's back. Other times he would sneak into the kitchen for a nap under the table. Duksit had his own house outside and grew a very thick coat of winter fur. He seemed to revel in the crisp air and would always greet us with a big grin, tail wagging.

Early the next year, Zimala had another baby—this time a bull calf. Momma said right from the start that we would not be able to keep "Teddy" because grown-up bulls could be dangerous. I did not argue against her position because I remembered an incident from the previous summer. I did not know why from time to time Mr. Christopherson let a bull in among his beef cattle. but when the bull was there, we were warned to stay out of that pasture.

One day Papa had Zimala on a rope, trying to lead her through a gate into the barnyard, but the bull was in the way and would not let them pass. He was acting as if Zimala belonged to him. Andrit was nearby with a stick in his hand and Papa was urging him to drive the bull out of the way. The bull had his head down and was drooling until the spittle dripped on the ground. His eyes rolled back and he emitted a dreadful bellow. It was a terrifying sight.

I was behind a fence and stood rooted to my spot and I could tell that Andrit was petrified. All of a sudden Max climbed through the fence and grabbed some small stones. Running forward he pelted the bull with the rocks. The bull started and brought his head up and then abandoned his power display and sauntered off to join his herd. Papa probably knew that he was a young bull and not really dangerous to us, but Andrit didn't know that, which is why he was so afraid. Max jumped up and down waving his arms at the retreating animal and chortled.

I thought about my brothers after that event and realized how different they were. I also thought about things that seem terrifying at first glance, but later might not be as bad as they seemed.

On some of those winter days I begged for a story from Momma's childhood. She started by saying that when she was a girl there were no barbed wire fences, so whenever the cows were out of the barn, someone had to watch them. Typically it was the youngest children since it did not require any strength or skill. Momma started:

> I remember a warm summer day when I was 11 or 12. The cows were grazing on the slope leading down to the creek and the sun was making me very drowsy. I had been herding since first light. One of the children always had to watch the cattle so that they would not stray into crop fields.
>
> Our bull, Dolars, was the first to lie down and start chewing his cud. He got extra feed so he was not as hungry as the rest of the herd. One by one the cows settled down in his vicinity. It occurred to me that I could lie down next to his warm brown back and take a little nap. When the herd gets up and moves away, he will get up to follow them and that will wake me, I thought.
>
> I sat down and leaned against him. Although he could be threatening to adults, especially strangers, he did not mind my presence. The fragrance of grass and flowers was all around and I was lulled to rest. I was so warm I fell into a deep sleep. Suddenly a voice jolted me awake. A neighbor who had come down to the creek to do laundry called out to me, "Little Shepherd, where are your cows!" I jumped up to see that Dolars is still dozing, but not another cow is to be seen. Heart pounding, I raced up the hill and in the distance I could see them, pillaging the garden.

Momma didn't remember whether she had gotten a spanking or just a talking to. I had never gotten an actual spanking, although once Max and I were splashing around in the little creek and did not hear Momma calling us to lunch. She was upset and slapped us on our bare butts as we ran up the trail to the house. It didn't hurt and after we ate lunch we took a nap. But I knew that Jurit had gotten more than one, and that Momma thought Papa was too severe. It caused conflict between the parents. Momma finally told Papa that she would take over disciplining the children and Papa said that was fine with him.

I had never seen a real spanking, but I understood it happened when you were older if you misbehaved. I was confident that I could discuss and negotiate any difficulties with Momma, so I was glad that she was in charge of that situation.

When Teddy was a few months old, our parents decided to give him to the Pilag family. They had to figure out how to get him there. Papa decided that if they took the rear seat out of Jurit's car, Teddy would fit in. They tied his legs together so that he could not jump around and settled him in a pile of straw. Jurit and Andrit got in and drove away. Everything went well and when they returned, they said that Teddy had weathered the trip just fine.

Around that time, Spolite surprised me by producing a litter of piglets. She had eight, I think, but every night for a while she inadvertently flattened one in her sleep. Eventually five survived and grew agile enough to get out of her way. They were black with a white collar around their shoulders, four boys and one girl. I leaned on the fence and watched their antics for hours.

When they were several months old, I went out to their pen and saw that Spolite was gone. I ran to tell Momma and she said that they had sold Spolite because pigs need a lot of food and she had grown enormous. She said the piglets were going to be sold as well in a while. "We have too many animals and they all need care and food and we just can't keep them all."

I didn't know that our parents were hoping to move somewhere where Papa could get a better job and that our menagerie needed to be cut down to a manageable size. I didn't know that the parents had tried to buy the house we lived in. Mr. Christopherson said he would only sell the whole place and not just the house (he wasn't ready to sell yet) and a few acres, but that we could live there as long as we wanted to.

I also did not know that they tried to buy a small farm near Vermillion with 14 acres of land and buildings that would house our cows and poultry. But that fell through as well because the sellers wanted a lot more for a down payment than my parents could raise. To me it was just another wonderful summer ahead with the brothers out of school and the promise that Ernina would be arriving soon.

South Dakota in the Rear View Mirror

I did not know that the summer of 1955 would be our last summer in South Dakota. It started off in a fine manner. Our parents planted a large garden. Momma pointed out the tiny plants as they emerged and explained what we would be eating in a few months—there were tasty things to look forward to. I was 5 ½, and even though no real work was expected of me, I tried to be helpful since an interest in making sure that the chickens had water or feed pleased Momma.

Aunt Erna would be arriving earlier this year and would spend another three months with us. Now that we had met her, we were even more excited about her impending visit. The Briedis children were not coming this summer because the family was expecting another child so they were all staying close to home. Our menagerie had shrunk over the winter—the ducks and turkeys were gone, as was Spolite and her family. There was still plenty to do and with the brothers out of school, Max and I were constant companions once again.

Tall green grass waved in the fields and the cattle got sleek again. Zimala munched the succulent grass and made more milk than we could use. Then, just when the garden was thriving and the mulberry bushes full of fruit and the apple trees loaded with small green apples, it stopped raining, A week went by and then two weeks. When a month went by without rain, Mr. Christopherson worried about the pasture drying up. He wondered whether there would be a corn crop that year.

Eventually he took his herd back to his place to be able to feed them hay. We started doing the same with Zimala and Parsla. My parents had bought hay the fall before, and we still had plenty left over. Later that summer it was impossible to buy hay since everyone needed it. Then it got hotter and hotter and everything green shriveled and dried up and fell to the ground. The trees lost their leaves. It looked like fall except that it was very hot.

The flower beds in the front yard that Momma had weeded and coaxed back into bloom over the previous two summers withered and died. The parents tried to keep the garden alive by hauling water in a barrel on a cart When Momma dug up some new potatoes and they were already cooked in the ground, she realized it was a lost cause.

Ernina arrived early in the drought and marveled that she had never seen anything like it. Papa went to work, so he had air conditioning during the day; Momma and Ernina were tired and listless unless we went to the pool. But the pool was so crowded that we didn't enjoy that much either.

The grass was so dry and sharp that Max and I had to give in and wear shoes when we went outside. The sound of birds chirping and singing vanished; our world grew quiet and very hot. During the day we spent time in what used to be the ice house. Built into the side of the hill, it was cooler, but it was also quite dark so there wasn't much I could do there except sit with Duksit and listen to Max chatting.

Late in the day when the sun eased up on beating the earth, I would take one of my stick horses and go for a ride around the farm. Max had no interest in horses so he did not usually accompany me. I kept them tied wherever there was a bit of shade and started leaving a pail of water so they could reach it. Their grass supply dwindled so I moved them often.

During this time Papa left on a trip. We didn't learn until later that he went to central Wisconsin to interview for a job. His journey went well and some time after he returned, he was offered the job and accepted it. I didn't know what to make of this major change. I kept asking Momma if Papa's new job would affect living on the farm. Gradually it became clear that we would have to move a great distance and would not be coming back to the farm.

Momma said later that it was probably a good thing that the summer had been so hot and dry because it made it easier to say goodbye to South Dakota. She also said that God had sent us to the very best place there could be to start our lives over in a new country. Now we had to move again and listen for his guidance in what would happen next.

I did not understand much about God except that Momma consulted him all the time by reading the Bible. There was a lot of traveling in the Bible stories they read to us so I knew it was not unusual for people to pick up and move. My most immediate concern was the animals and how we would move them to our new home. It never occurred to me that they would not accompany us; fortunately, that did not occur to my parents either.

The next several weeks were a blur of activity while the parents packed and decided what to take along. We also visited folks we knew to say goodbye. The bigger people were stressed and grumpy so Max and I tried to stay out of the way.

I learned that Papa's new boss had offered us his guesthouse for the winter, rent free. Papa said there were some other sheds around the guesthouse and that we could probably temporarily house our animals there.

I think that our parents got exasperated with my endless questions about Zimala and Parsla's future welfare. I did get Momma to promise that there would be a home for them and that we would have them with us just like we did here in South Dakota. I did not get it in writing (I could neither read nor write), but Momma was trustworthy as far as I was concerned.

Duksit and Mintz were virtually family members so there was no issue about them coming along and hanging out with us. But even at five, I could see that transporting and maintaining cattle was a much larger problem.

It was September and it had not rained for 70 days when a large semi drove into our yard. The driver announced that we would need to load our possessions onto it. He would then drive everything to Wisconsin for us. The parents showed him what we wanted to move: the kitchen stove, a wringer washer, a couple beds, kitchen supplies, two bicycles (we had outgrown the tricycles and gave them away), and various odds and ends. Our household goods did not amount to much. When they showed him the two cows, a couple cages of rabbits, and chickens, he looked doubtful. He explained that his truck was not meant for hauling large animals. The parents' predicament affected him—and there was a window in the truck—so he said he would talk to his boss.

He drove away and returned a while later to say that the boss had given him the go-ahead. He left the trailer, saying he would return early the next morning to start the journey. He had backed it up to a slight rise so that it would be possible for us to get the cows up onto it. Papa and Jurit made a pen for the cows out of bales of hay and then boxed in a small barrel so that the animals would have access to water. They made a ramp from more hay bales and Zimala walked up rather gingerly, offering no resistance. Parsla practically jumped in, perhaps concerned that she might be left behind.

I brought the wooden animals I had made the previous fall and we loaded them as well. When the family went in to supper, I gathered my other horse collection. I piled them near the back of the trailer and waited for Papa. He came out with a few more things to put inside and asked, "What is this pile of sticks doing here?" I was disappointed in his inability to see the herd of beautiful horses that the sticks represented. Even after I explained everything to him, he said, "We are not taking all these sticks—you can choose three, but the rest have to stay behind."

It was hard to decide which three to take, but eventually I made my choice and Papa put them on the truck. I took the rest back behind the apple orchard and laid them down in the grass. I untied them and removed all the binder twine. I told them they were on their own and would have to find their own food and water. I stayed with them until the sun was setting, when I finally went into the house.

When I got up the next morning, the truck was gone. Momma said the driver arrived very early and headed out. It was barely light when we had a quick breakfast and loaded the two cars. Max and I and Mintz rode with Momma and Papa in our car. Jurit drove his car with Andrit and Ernina and Duksit. We made some stops along the way, so it was dark when we arrived at our destination. We had traveled over 500 miles from South Dakota to central Wisconsin!

It had gotten much cooler and greener as we traveled north. The scent of pine needles and the shushing of the wind through the branches greeted us at our new home. The guesthouse, at the end of a long, private drive, was surrounded by large pine trees and a forest that went on in all directions. We were very tired and found a bed and slept. Our parents, exhausted from the move, appreciated the next day which was quiet and cool. That evening the truck driver arrived and all the men set up a ramp again with hay bales and unloaded the cows. They led them in to one of the sheds and tied them. When Momma talked to them in Latvian, they relaxed. She then milked Zimala while Ernina served the truck driver some pancakes for supper.

Our parents asked him how the trip went. The driver said, "You told me that sometime during the trip I would have to milk the cow to relieve the pressure in her udder. I figured that would be no problem." He went on to recount that when he stopped at a wayside he heard Zimala start to bellow. He climbed into the back of the truck to try to milk her. He said he applied all the pressure to the teats that his hands could produce; nothing happened. Sweat was pouring from his brow and his back was soaked and the cow just kept bellowing. He was starting to feel desperate when a woman who had also stopped at the wayside came to the back of the truck.

She asked him what the problem was. He explained and she said, "I will milk the cow for you." He helped her into the truck and she showed him how to do it. In a couple minutes, she had released enough milk to stop Zimala's bellowing. The driver said, "I don't know what I would have done if she hadn't come over to help me." Later Papa translated the story to Ernina, who laughed and laughed. "That poor man," she said, "but thankfully they all made the trip safely."

A day or two later Papa's boss stopped by to see how we were doing and commented on all the animals we had brought. He said that the winters are very cold with usually lots of snow. He wasn't sure that the shed would provide enough shelter for the cows. But for now, September was marvelously cool and we all felt refreshed. In a clearing, Papa and Jurit made a fenced-in area where the cows could graze during the day. In the evening, they were led back to the shed and tied inside overnight.

I usually went along when it was time to bring the cows home. One evening I went with Jurit. He put a halter on Zimala without any trouble, but Parsla was another matter. By now she had small horns and she kept tossing her head and ducking so that Jurit could not get the halter on her. I went up to her and reached over her neck and took a horn in each hand and pulled her head down. In her ear I said, "Izbeidz," Latvian for *knock it off.* She stood quietly then and Jurit got the halter on her. He held onto her lead. Zimala knew where we were going and made a beeline for the shed, but Parsla could not be trusted to do the same if she wasn't controlled by a rope.

My brothers were all enrolled in school again. Jurit would drop off Andrit and Max on his way to high school. Max did not like his new school any better than the old one in South Dakota and his recalcitrance showed. His teacher told our parents at parent-teacher conferences that she thought he was "retarded." They weren't sure what that meant, but it became a source of amusement for his siblings for many years to come. Andrit went from a class of two to a large classroom, but he said he was ahead in some subjects because of all the personal attention he got from Mrs. Smith. He loved to read, so he did well in school.

A couple weeks after we arrived in Wisconsin, Ernina had to return to Canada. We all went with her to the local train station to see her off. We badgered her about whether she would come again the next summer. She wasn't sure, she said, because "it is hard to find a new job every year, so I might have to wait a while before I can make the trip again."

With everyone gone during the day and Momma busy in the house, Duksit and I explored the woods. There were clearings every so often and with the sun warming the ground Duksit and I could sit on the cushion of pine needles and look around. When I got tired I would just say *maja* to Duksit and he would lead me home. Duksit was not tied up and would sometimes explore the woods on his own. One day he did not come home for supper. The next day I called and called his name and scanned the woods for a glimpse of his tawny coat and waving tail. I could not concentrate on anything and wandered around the yard visiting with the other animals but feeling desolate at the same time.

Momma tried to reassure me that dogs sometimes wandered for a few days but that he would come home again when he was hungry. The following day we called some more and then in the far distance we could hear a dog barking. When Papa came home we told him what we had heard; maybe Duksit was tangled in some brush because the barking started when Momma called his name. Papa and Jurit set out to see if they could find him. They called Duksit's name and followed the sound into the forest.

It was dark and a long time later when they returned to the house. Papa was carrying Duksit and Jurit was supporting his right front paw and the steel trap attached to it. They laid him down in the kitchen. It had taken them a long time to get home because Duksit was heavy and they had to switch off carrying the dog and carrying the trap. They tried not to hurt him, but in the dark they could not figure out how to free him. So they pulled up the stake that chained the trap to the ground and brought everything home. Papa said trappers are supposed to check their traps every day; it was a terrible thing to leave an animal caught in that cruel way.

It did not take long in the light of the kitchen for them to get the trap off. Momma was aghast at such a torture device. Papa took the trap outside and I never saw it again. Momma made a bed from an old blanket near the kitchen stove and Duksit crawled onto it. She set a large bowl of scraps and warm milk within his reach and he gobbled it all down. His paw was swollen and Papa said he might have some broken bones and they would have to see how it healed. After his meal, Duksit licked and licked his injury.

He looked a little sheepish and over the next couple days, as I sat next to him and carefully stroked his head, we had long talks about staying around the yard and not wandering off by himself. By the third day he would not come inside anymore and slept in his doghouse instead. It was packed with fresh hay and had a canvas flap to cover the opening. Mintz often went in and curled up with his pal. Duksit kept his paw up for a couple weeks and hopped around on three legs before he started using it again. He had a slight limp on that side for the rest of his life, but it did not hinder his activities.

Momma had a lot of daily tasks. The house had no indoor plumbing, so Momma had to use a hand pump and carry water from a well in the yard. Papa and Jurit tried to fill up all the large containers ahead of time, but sometimes she needed more, especially when she did the laundry. Because we had no bathroom, baths were a makeshift operation. The outhouse was connected to the cabin by a breezeway, so it wasn't as cold as having to go completely outside, but it still wasn't a place you could dawdle.

Sometime that fall the parents bought a black and white console television. During the day Momma tuned in to the one channel we could receive. One day she was so engrossed in a program that she let the pan holding the ground beef casserole tip and it slid out of her grip and crashed to the floor. Duksit got a major treat that day. She thought the soap operas would have some resolution, but after several months of watching, she realized that would never happen. But watching TV did improve Momma's ability to speak English and to understand it.

On weekends we watched variety shows as a family, but Saturday afternoon broadcasts of *Little Rascals* became a magnet for Max and me. I especially enjoyed the goat hitched to a small wagon. Momma just had to call out that name from the door and we would come running from wherever we happened to be. *The Lone Ranger* and *Hopalong Cassidy* also became great favorites. I studied the horses and dreamed about having one of my own.

In November it got colder. Snow fell and did not melt. The cows grew long thick hair, but it was clear that they were cold in their little three-sided shed. The parents started to fret about what to do with them over the winter because they now realized that Wisconsin winters were different from South Dakota's. When Papa had started his job, stories about the chemist who brought his cows with him circulated around the company. When Papa explained his problem at the office, one of his colleagues said that maybe his parents could take them for the winter. They had just sold their herd and retired from years of dairy farming but still had lots of feed and a barn.

In short order, the arrangements were made; a truck came and took Parsla and Zimala away. The deal was that the folks taking the cows would keep whatever milk Zimala gave and they would get to keep the calf that she would have in a month or so. I was reassured by Momma that we would find a place where we could all be together by the next summer.

More snow fell and the woods filled up with drifts so we couldn't do much exploring any more. During the day I was confined to the drive except when Momma had time to go out on our road for a walk. Sometimes she pulled me along on a sled. One day we decided to make a little harness and hitch up Duksit. He pulled me back and forth along the snow packed road. I got chilly long before Duksit wanted to give up his new job.

One winter evening when Jurit brought his brothers home from school, Momma noticed that Max was shivering. His pants were soaking wet so she told him to take them off and she would get him some dry clothes. When he pulled down his pants and underwear I saw that his butt was completely blue which frightened me. I thought he was injured. Momma checked and said the dye from his wet jeans had transferred to his skin. As she fixed a bath for him, she questioned Andrit and Max. We learned that while waiting for Jurit, Max had slid down the hill near their school on his bottom. He thought that was fun and kept doing it until Jurit arrived.

The winter passed quickly and what I remember most is that Max and I shared chicken pox. But that malady passed too and soon the days were longer and the temperature moderated. Our landlord, Dr. Schepfel, invited us to his home a few times. He also paid us to dust the many objects on every flat surface. He had grown up in Austria and came to America before the war and had many mementos from his earlier life. I am not sure how diligent we were, but he paid us and gave us milk and cookies. Money meant nothing to me, but Max was happy to take my share too. The cookies were quite tasty though and I probably got more than my share.

Dr. Shepfel's house, built close to the Wisconsin River, was made from large logs. It had high ceilings and a fine view from his living room. The interior of his house was fascinating although a little creepy. Heads of various animals—magnificent deer and elk and bears and others that I could not identify—were hanging from the walls. Whenever I was there, I felt those dead animals were watching me.

Our parents, realizing the need to find a permanent home, started looking at houses that they might be able to buy. Realtors showed various city houses, some of them quite close to where Papa worked. At first I thought these excursions were fun until I realized that if we moved to one of those houses set on a tiny (by my standards) scrap of land, there would be no place for the cows.

I started whining about the size of the yards and pointed out there would be no room for a proper garden. But Momma argued that Papa could walk to work and the schools and a small grocery store were close by. As these outings continued, the awful realization sank in to my small brain that we could actually end up living in a city. I grew desperate.

Years later when I had a career as a lawyer, I learned that when all of your arguments failed to move the jury (or more often the judge) you could "throw in the kitchen sink"—say something outrageous and desperate—to try to slow the juggernaut about to roll over your client.

I didn't know anything about such theories in the early spring of 1956, but my feelings of desperation were very clear. Finally, one day I threw a tantrum. I cried and stamped my feet and yelled at my mother. She looked dismayed when I told her that had I known that she would break her promise about a place for the cows, I would not have left South Dakota. I would have stayed there.... with the cows. Emotions struggled on her face—as if she didn't know whether to laugh or cry.

When I had calmed down, Momma said that she and Papa didn't really want to live in a city either, but they had to do what was best for the family. About that time, the outdoor pump that we relied on malfunctioned and Dr. Schepfel called a plumber. That is how we met Oscar Rockman. Momma said later that God sent him to help us find a place to live in the country.

The Farm on Spring Road

It was probably late March when we started expeditions to the country. Realtors took us to several small, run-down, sometimes abandoned, farms. I don't remember any of the houses, but Momma said some were not habitable. I do remember the barns because I would make a beeline to explore them and invariably could see they were not suitable. Some were tilted on their foundations or had cracks in the walls or you could see all the way up to the sky through the rotten roofs. I would inform Momma of my findings.

My parents were getting discouraged so when Mr. Rockman came to fix the pump, they told him about their problem. He told them that he knew all the small farms in the area and which ones were for sale. One day he drove us to the farm on Spring Road. The adults went to meet the owners and view the house and, as usual, I headed right for the barn. Animals had not been housed there for many years, but the walls were straight and the doors tight. The roof was in order and all the windows had glass. The animal part of the barn on the left had two sections—two large stalls in the front (which housed work horses) and a large section with stanchions and some small pens in the back.

A large drive-through area in the middle accommodated the tractor, hay wagon, and hay loader. The barn frame, made of large beams, was still straight and true. The right side had a granary and a storage area and beyond that was an attached garage. I was very pleased that the barn was in good order, and I whispered that to Momma when I got a chance.

Our parents loved the place right away. It was on a hill and had a great view. Although the house was small and did not have indoor plumbing, they were not discouraged. They were confident that they could make improvements to make it comfortable. Berta and Andrew Golkoski had lived there a long time (she had been born on the farm). Her father had cleared the land and although she said it was never very successful because there were lots of rocks and the soil was not very good, they had kept dairy cows, had a large garden, and had survived. Mr. Golkoski, who worked in a paper mill, had decided to build a house with "all the conveniences" closer to town.

The farm had been on the market for quite a while and had no takers. We were eager to buy it. Papa asked Dr. Schepfel to review the documents. He looked at the sale contract and recommended that we wait a few months until the contract with the realtor expired. The Golkoskis were agreeable because they would not have to pay a commission; they were willing to reduce the price. The final price for the 80-acre farm and the farm implements was $7,500.

The farm had a separate building that used to be a granary that had been remodeled. It now had one large room with a wood stove at one end and room for several beds at the other. In between was a dining and sitting area. Mrs. Golkoski's father had lived out his life in that "little house" and had died recently. His death precipitated their decision to move off the farm.

We reached an agreement whereby we would move to the farm. Most of us would live in the little house, although the big brothers soon opted to sleep on the hay mow. Eventually, they also gave us a bedroom in the main house and Max and I moved in there.

I don't remember how we moved to the farm, but I do remember the day in early May when the cows were delivered. The world had that soft green color of spring and the scent of apple blossoms wafted on the breeze. The truck driver pulled into a fenced-in area by the barn and let down the ramp. Zimala, nervous and uncertain, came down first; Parsla crowded right behind her. Momma spoke to them in Latvian and called them into the barn where she had placed some treats in the horse trough. Zimala's ears came down and the fur on her neck settled back into place (if a cow could let out a big sigh, Zimala did it that day). They knew they were home again. I knew that all was right with my world.

Momma had decided that the cows were going to stay in the front part in the stalls that had been made for work horses. They were wider and longer and had a wood floor so the cows would be warmer when they lay down. Momma said that stanchions were torture instruments and when we owned the farm, she would have Papa tear them out and throw them on a rock pile.

The cows were tied with light chains that ended in a Y that looped around their necks and closed when the bar at one end was put through the ring at the other and turned sideways. The weight of the chain kept it in place, but it was also easy to open when letting the cows outside. The long end of the chain was secured to the wall. Zimala and Parsla learned their places quickly and would not allow the other one in their spot.

The return of the cows meant more work for Momma. She did the milking twice a day, processed the milk, and made all the things we enjoyed. It meant fewer expenses at the grocery store. We would have to save every single cent that summer so that we would have the money to buy the farm.

My brothers were still in school. Andrit and Max now went to a nearby two-room country school and Jurit attended high school in Mosinee. He dropped off his brothers on the way. Mr. Golkoski and Papa went to work and sometimes Mrs. Golkoski went on errands of her own after dropping off Mr. Golkoski at the factory.

I accompanied Momma on all her daily tasks although I probably missed some since I liked to sleep in. We fed the animals, gathered the eggs, and made sure the rabbits had food and water. Mrs. Golkoski showed us where we could plant a garden; after Papa worked up the soil, Momma got busy with that project. Spring in Wisconsin was truly lovely. The pale green of new grass and leaves was punctuated by apple and wild cherry blossoms. The scent of blooming lilacs was intoxicating; every day I spent some time with my face buried in the branches of the lilac bushes.

The highlight of the day for Momma was when the mailman drove up to the box by the road and delivered mail. Whenever there was a letter from Ernina, she would sit right down and read it. I would watch her face as she absorbed news about the homeland. She would then tell me bits and pieces about what she had learned.

One fine spring afternoon, we were in the living room of the farm where Momma sat reading a letter from Ernina. All of a sudden Momma's face got dark, and she fell to the floor on her knees. She clutched her head, sobbing and moaning. I was terrified and ran to her trying to comfort her. She pushed me away forcefully and said, "You can't understand, you can't understand." I retreated to a chair in the corner of the room. I had never seen my mother so distraught so I didn't know what to do. Slowly her words made some sense, her sobbing eased, and she explained that her mother, Mimite, had died.

Eventually she went into the bedroom that Max and I used and closed the door. I listened at the door and could hear her crying. I went outside, I called Duksit, and the two of us went for a walk around the yard and out into the pasture. He could sense my worry; he licked my hand and stayed close. Eventually we found a rock pile that had a big flat rock at the top which was warmed by the sun. I climbed up and sat and looked around at the marvelous view. I could not imagine a world without Momma in it so I did not want to think about how Momma felt now that her mother was gone.

Later when everyone came home, I told the brothers what had happened. Papa told us that Momma was very tired and had gone to bed and that he would make pancakes for supper. Papa also milked the cow; the brothers helped with other animal care tasks. Jurit looked sad—he remembered Mimite when they were all together in the homeland. The next morning Momma was up and doing her usual tasks, but she was not her usual energetic self.

After Mimite died I realized that I would never meet any of my grandparents, but I remained curious about them. The curiosity grew as I got older. Papa remembered very little about his parents, but Momma had a much longer relationship with hers, so she had many more stories. Several that had a profound effect on my life were vignettes about how my grandparents related to other people, particularly those who were somehow different from them.

When we were children, Momma told us many times her beliefs about the source of our good fortune. She firmly believed that our family always had shelter during the War and major assistance whenever we needed it because her parents had always treated strangers kindly. She said that Mimite and Andrejs Kalnins never turned anyone away who needed food or shelter. Momma felt that their willingness to help the less fortunate benefited all their children later in life.

Grandfather Andrejs, who never cared for farm work, ended up living in the country after the revolution in 1905; there was a revolt against German control of Latvia and a great deal of destruction was done. Many beautiful manor houses, built by the German owners, were burnt to the ground. Although Grandfather refused to participate in the chaos, he was powerless to stop it. He had been trained and enjoyed his work as a telegraph operator. When the rebellion destroyed the telegraph offices and lines, he was out of a job. Newly married with a small child, he had to seek other employment; he ended up at the Inn and Tavern which eventually became the family home.

He started out working in the stable taking care of horses lodged there by travelers. Later the bar manager retired and talked him into taking over the Tavern. The basement had liquor left over from when the German Barons had owned the business and now he would have to pay rent to the County instead. He didn't do well as a bartender (he let too many people drink on credit and then had trouble collecting the bills). Eventually he went out of business and had to sell some livestock to pay *his* debts.

Just about that time, World War I had started and he was drafted into the Russian army. Russia was trying to gain the upper hand in the Baltic States and that part of Latvia was occupied at various times by the Russians and the Germans. When the War was over and Latvia had acquired its freedom, veterans were allotted property formerly owned by German landholders. That is how my grandparents acquired the Inn/Tavern (although it had not been used as such for some time) and some surrounding land.

Momma said her father much preferred other kinds of work. Although he had no formal training in that area, he often went to Riga where he performed tasks that a lawyer might do. He was always interested in everyone he encountered. Momma said that when she drove to town with him, he would leave her in the wagon to guard the purchases and watch the horse while he did various errands. She would see him coming back down the street, stopping every few feet to visit with someone. It took him a long time to get back to the wagon.

Mimite, on the other hand, was shy and preferred the quiet life of the country. There was often conflict between them about how often Grandfather should be away on other missions. He never got paid much, but he could never turn down a request for help. When it came to basic values and what they taught their children, however, they were very much in agreement.

Although independence in 1918 was thrilling for Latvians, it was a traumatic time for others living there. Momma remembered that some years after the First World War ended, a young Russian couple came to her father begging for help. They had heard that he would help people who needed documents prepared and that he knew his way around the bureaucracy in Riga. The Czar had settled them in Latvia some years previously. They had since built a small house and barn and had several small children. Terrified that they were going to be evicted, they did not know where they would go.

Momma said her father calmed them down, gathered the information he needed, and wrote a petition on their behalf. She remembered her father's beautiful handwriting—almost like calligraphy—(he wrote with a quill pen). He then took the document to Riga, and had the title to their farm affirmed, so they did not need to move.

A homeless person named John came by from time to time in the winter. An old man, with long white hair and beard, he would not speak unless an adult asked him a question. Most of the time, he just sat with his head down. Momma said he seemed to be talking to himself under his breath. Sometimes when he arrived, he would be covered with frost, his beard frozen. He would come into the kitchen and sit on a low masonry wall near the stove through which smoke passed on its way out of the building. It was always warm there. When John stopped by, Grandmother would set up a mattress filled with straw, give him some blankets, and he would spend the night.

Grandmother would also feed him, give him new socks and mittens, and food for the road. He never stayed for more than one night at a time. Since there was no easy way to take a bath in those days, he always brought lice with him. In spite of the lice, the Grandparents never turned him away.

A variety of Jewish tradesman stopped by the farm to sell or buy various things. Momma remembered one occasion when an old Jewish man, a rag picker, drove into the yard. He would buy old rags, throw them on his wagon, and drive them to a place that recycled them into horse blankets and similar things. A couple young women who were laborers on the farm snickered at the rag man. Grandfather walked up to them and told them there was nothing to laugh about. The rag picker was an old man who could not do heavy work and this was his way of making a living. He did not steal and he was not a beggar, so there was nothing to laugh about. He admonished that he did not want to hear them ever doing that again. Her father's words made a strong impression on Momma who was nearby at the time.

Momma said that her parents never tolerated any anti-Semitic talk or derogatory comments about Jews or any people. They taught their children to treat all people with respect. Momma said in light of what happened in Europe, she was very glad that her parents had understood what was so very important for a Christian society to know.

Another event that Momma remembered: Milda, the horse who had escaped the requisition during the War while Grandfather was away, grew old and finally feeble. Because her teeth had worn down to stubs, she had trouble eating. They fed her ground feed mixed in warm water so she could just drink her nourishment but their efforts to save Milda failed. Grandfather got in touch with some men who dug a hole and buried her beyond the apple orchard. On her way home from school, Momma noticed the newly turned mound of dirt. The men who dug the grave marveled that Andrejs Kalnins had Milda buried without taking off her hide. Such a hide could bring 10 *lats*!

A day or two later, a gypsy came to the farm and said he had heard about the horse that had been buried with its hide on. He begged Grandfather to let him dig her up. He said, "It will rot anyway and I have a family to feed." Grandfather did not want to disturb Milda's grave, but eventually Mimite talked him in to it. "Milda does not need it; this man obviously does," she said. Grandfather relented. The gypsy worked alone and reburied the horse after he was done.

From a very early age, Grandfather taught Momma to sit by him and read the Bible out loud. He said that although she did not understand it all now, she would when she was older, and she should just keep reading. Momma said that her father's efforts to introduce her to the wisdom contained in the Bible proved to be very important. The Bible was the polestar of her life.

Although Momma was sad for a long time after getting the letter about Mimite's death, there was so much to do around the farm and it was such a beautiful place that it had a cheering effect. She worked in the garden every chance she got. I could see her relax in the early summer sun as she looked at the small growing plants.

Unlike in South Dakota where we just bought baled hay, we would have to make our own hay now because the winters were long, and we could not afford to buy it. Papa and Jurit spent time figuring out how the implements worked with the help of Mr. Golkoski. In July, Papa mowed the hay field in the middle of the woods that made up the second forty-acre parcel. Jurit drove the tractor, and with Andrit sitting on the rake, they pulled the sweet-smelling dry hay into windrows. After that, Jurit drove the tractor and Papa and Andrit rode on the wagon, stacking the hay as it came up the hay loader.

The loose hay had to be stacked properly and stomped down so that it did not slide off the wagon. When the mound was higher than the mouth of the hay loader, they would unhitch the loader and drive home along the roads that bordered our property. I remember watching the process from the edge of the field and then running home through the woods to beat them to the barn.

They would pull the wagon into the drive-through area, unhitch the tractor, and then drive around to the front side of the barn. Papa used a special fork attached to a rope that ran on pulleys up to a track in the roof of the barn. The tractor pulled the other end of the rope and lifted the hay and moved it along the track. The load ran along the track to either side of the hay mow.

Pulling another rope released the levers holding the hay to the fork and it fell into a big mound. After they unloaded the wagon, they had to be spread out the hay in the mow so that it would continue to dry and cool. Too much warm hay in one area could start a fire! It was very laborious and dusty work.

Years later when I did more of the work that was involved with the haying process, I often operated the fork and learned that it was tricky to stick enough hay, but not so much as to start to lift the whole wagon. Haying season was a stressful time because it was important to get it in before it got rained on. The animals got more nutrition from hay dried properly and cut while still tender and leafy.

In August the realty contract expired; it was time to buy the farm. However, problems surfaced. Mrs. Golkoski informed us that some of her Chicago relatives might want to buy it. The parents were shocked and dismayed. But Momma calmed everyone by saying that God had led us here, and if it was his plan that we have the farm, then things would work out.

After a couple weeks, the Golkoskis told us that the relatives had decided they did not want the farm after all. We could go ahead with the purchase. When the parents went to the bank, they were surprised to learn that they would need to come up with a $3,000 down payment before the bank would lend the rest. The bankers cited the fact that we were new to the area and that Papa had only worked in Wisconsin for a year.

Momma gathered all our resources. She emptied all the piggy banks, searched jacket pockets, and scraped the bottom of her purse. Jurit threw in what cash he had. When every single cent was counted, the parents had $2,500 and no idea how to raise any more. Papa told his colleague Clarence about our problem. Clarence told him to talk to the company financial officer.

When Papa explained the situation, the officer said, "We don't do this ordinarily, but given your circumstances, the company will advance the money from your salary. We will deduct it from your paycheck. By Christmas it will be paid back." At that time, Papa earned $450 a month and knew it would not be a problem to pay it back so quickly. He thanked the financial manager profusely.

I was not privy to all the document signing, but I do remember the relieved expressions on Momma and Papa's faces when the farm was officially theirs. For the first time in their lives, the parents owned their own home! Papa turned 46 that fall and Momma 41. I overheard them talking about how they hoped they would never have to move again.

The Golkoskis stayed on the farm for a couple more months while their house was being built. The adults got along very amicably. Mrs. Golkoski baked pies and exceptionally fine peanut butter cookies. I liked to hang around the kitchen when she was baking since she would leave a plate of cookies on the kitchen table and tell us to help ourselves.

By Christmas time, their new house was ready and they moved away. I could tell that Mrs. Golkoski felt sad about leaving. She had been born there and lived there her whole life. Momma said she should come to visit whenever she wanted. Momma also suggested that she should take some lilac bushes to their new house. We remained friendly with them for the rest of their lives. Momma recently passed to me the springtime task of planting fresh flowers in the urns by their graves.

Liberty School

That fall, when I was six-years-and-almost-nine-months old, I joined my youngest brothers at Liberty School. Getting up early was never a preferred activity, but the excitement of the new adventure got me up that first day without any trouble.

Momma braided my hair and dressed me in going-to-school clothes (which were new and not as comfortable as my worn, soft summer, cotton ones). When Jurit dropped us off, Max showed me the way since we were going to be in the same classroom. A two-room school with grades one through four in one room and five through eight in the other, the whole school had maybe 25 students—four of us in the first grade. Although Max was just 16 months older, he was two grades ahead of me because his birthday was in mid September. He had started school when he was almost six. He sat in the third-grade row and we did not interact much until recess.

Our teacher, Mrs. Reidel, was jovial and kind. She told us that we would start learning our letters so that we could then learn to read and write. In the first couple weeks, I realized that I already knew how to read. I had absorbed the knowledge at home, but no one had ever told me that I could read. There was a bookshelf in the back of the room that was our "library." Mrs. Reidel did not force me to participate in learning activities with the other students as they labored over their letters; she let me read undisturbed. I would fill out the little workbooks and do the arithmetic problems, but most of the days I spent reading my way through the bookshelf.

She did insist that we go outside for recess and at lunch time. When it rained or got too cold, the whole school would go downstairs to the basement and play *pom pom pull away* and various other games. Pom pom pullaway involved two teams lined up and holding hands. Little kids were placed between bigger stronger ones. Each team took turns calling a particular child to "come over." That kid would run at the line and try to break through. If successful, he or she could pick anyone of the broken line team to come back to the other side. If the line held, the runner would have to join that side. There was some strategy required since the little kids were easy to hold, but then they could also be weak links. The game ended when a pitiful few were left on one side or, more often, when the lunch hour was over. Mrs. Reidel and the other teacher would take part right along with the students. I remember its being a great deal of fun.

I don't remember any problems at school other than my growing concern about getting more books to read. By spring, I had finished reading all the books in our room. About that time, the Bookmobile (a converted school bus that was a library for country schools) started stopping at our school. We were allowed to select two books which would be due in two weeks when the Bookmobile came around again. The Bookmobile selection was considerable. I tried to negotiate for more books, but the librarian would not budge. Two books per student was the limit. I read mine in three days.

As I was getting off the Bookmobile one day, chagrined at all the books that were going to be wasted since I would not be able to read them, I noticed Max and several small boys running around a nearby field throwing rocks at each other. This scene became an inspiration.

The next time the Bookmobile came, I had talked Max and several other boys to come on the bus with me and check out the two books I gave to each of them. When we went into the building, I collected the books from the boys, read them, and returned them when they were due. The librarian made some comments about the boys' sudden interest in reading. But they all maintained the silence I had impressed on them; they did not thwart my plan.

That winter, I missed a whole month of school with the mumps (first on one side of my neck and then on the other). Mrs. Reidel told my mother that ordinarily a student would be held back to do the grade over, but since I was well ahead of my grade level, there would be no need to do that.

I think that my wish to always have something to read was based on the need to escape into worlds where things turned out okay and where the animal heroes overcame every difficulty. I never liked to talk or think about traumatic events.

In February of 1957, Zimala had a female calf whose father was a jersey, so she was small and brown with some white markings. She ended up with the name Brunite (Brownie). The parents did not intend to keep her (they already had two cows and that was plenty). But one Saturday morning, shortly after Brownie was born, I awoke to upset voices and my parents and Jurit going in and out of the barn. We young ones were strictly forbidden to go out there. Eventually we learned that a freak accident had claimed Zimala's life.

When a truck came into the yard, Jurit told us that it had come to take Zimala away. We couldn't see anything from the house, but could hear Parsla mooing for her mother—a sort of questioning moo—as if to ask, "Where are you?"

Later Momma explained what had happened. The evening before, she had given the cows cut-up potatoes and beets as a treat. Apparently, Zimala had been reaching in to Parsla's share of the trough and had lost her balance and had fallen into the trough. In her struggles to get up and out, she had ended up on her back and suffocated. Without human intervention, she was trapped, still tied by her neck chain and held in by the wall of the trough. Momma's face told me that it was a terrible scene. I never wanted to think about how long it took her to die or how poor Parsla felt watching her mother expire.

That day, the parents moved Parsla into the back of the barn. Jurit and Papa took turns with the sledge hammer knocking out the concrete trough, removing the pieces. Then they built mangers that were off the ground with v-shaped openings that no cow could ever fall into. Parsla was moved back into her place (she kept calling for Zimala).

By the next weekend, when I was allowed to go to the barn, things had settled down. Parsla had started communicating with little Brownie and was adjusting to life without her mother. My parents beat themselves up over the accident for a long time; they felt that they should have foreseen the danger. I started to think that the ones I loved best were most likely to die, but I did not share my thoughts with anyone.

In the weeks ahead, I spent extra time with Brownie brushing her and making sure that she was well bedded since she was now an orphan. She had a compliant and sweet personality much like her mother. Her fur was silky and she was always gentle and friendly. I spent a lot of time in her pen. The empty spot where Zimala had stood was hard to look at, so I busied myself with other tasks.

In the long run, Zimala's misfortune was good fortune for Brownie. She lived out her 24 years on the farm and died when Papa had to put her down. She had gotten very arthritic in the knees and had trouble with her balance and with grazing. She spent the last summer of her life on the lawn eating the soft grass and resting where she wanted to. But often she couldn't get up without help. Papa would brace her rear end so that she could get her front legs straightened out. My parents decided that there was no point in putting her through another winter.

But I didn't know how all that would turn out the spring of my seventh year. The season of new things came around again with blooming trees and new grass. Parsla had her own calf which was sold after a few months. Brownie and Parsla roamed the pasture together and life settled in to a summer routine. Papa bought a wooden boat with a motor and made a trailer so that he could explore some of Wisconsin's lakes. He usually brought home fresh fish which the rest of us loved to eat.

On weekends, we often traveled to Crooked Lake where Papa put the boat in the water and went fishing. Max often went along but the rest of us usually stayed on shore. Sometimes Andrit stayed home because he preferred to read. I think Jurit came along a few times, but he had other things he wanted to do as well. The lake had sparkling clear water and lily pads along the shore. Beneath them, you could see various types of fish. Max, always looking for the existence of aquatic life, spotted them first.

Sometimes Momma went into the pine woods and found wild mushrooms. She could tell the edible ones from the poisonous ones and we had many feasts flavored by her forest harvest.

I learned to swim that summer, but I didn't get to read as much as I wanted to because Max was a man of action. He nagged me to accompany him on explorations of the farm and the woods and even all the way to the little creek on a neighbor's property that was about a mile from our house. We saw flowers and bushes and trees that were very different from what had grown in South Dakota. Max was convinced that somewhere on the farm there should be a stream that might hold fish. Although we found stagnant pools in the marshy areas, we did not find any running water.

Duksit accompanied us on our expeditions. When we came home, Papa showed us how to brush him and to look for wood ticks which we would throw into a can of water. Duksit was very patient as we explored his fur. In the prime of his life, he enjoyed the freedom of his large yard and farm. But every so often, other needs, which we did not understand, caused him to disappear for a few days at a time. Sometimes he came home with cuts and injuries to his face and ears. Papa said he was out looking for girlfriends. Years later Momma said he should have been neutered, but no one thought about such things then. Even the vet who gave him the rabies shot once a year did not suggest it.

In our daily trips into the woods, I do not remember being bothered by mosquitoes. The light filtering through the trees made a magical place on the forest floor. I found small delicate flowers of various colors and in some clearings we found tiny wild strawberries. We learned to recognize blackberries and when they were ripe ate them by the handful.

Mrs. Golkoski came by with her sister Louise to pick them as well. Sometimes Momma went out and picked pails full for them so they wouldn't have to work so hard. But they enjoyed going into the woods and told Momma that they looked forward to it. I enjoyed their visits because Mrs. Golkoski invariably brought baked treats with her, often peanut butter cookies.

Later in the summer our parents bought their first new car, a 1957 Ford Fairlane with a V-8 engine. It was cream and gold with large fins on the back. They also started home improvement projects. They knocked out the wall between the two tiny bedrooms on the west side of the house and made a bigger room which eventually became the music room and held the piano and the stereo. They installed an indoor bathroom with a tub so our bath time was very comfortable and much easier for Momma to manage.

There was another big garden that year, but, as usual, I did not have to do any garden work. Momma showed me the difference between the young carrot plants and the weeds. I pulled two or three, but quickly lost interest in assuming the bent-over position needed for the work. Momma worked for hours tending the garden—early in the morning or late in the day when it was not too hot.

She told me that when she was a child, she was sent out into the garden to weed and otherwise work there because she was too small to handle the heavy cooking utensils and too weak to help with milking the cows. She also said she liked being in the garden as that was one of her jobs from early childhood. Now, as an adult, she loved dealing with plants and flowers and watching them grow and bring fruit. Our parents often talked about how the peace of the farm seemed like paradise to them after all the turmoil of the War and the anxiety of moving to America. For Momma, that peace was multiplied whenever she was in the garden.

Momma noticed Max's intense interest with anything having to do with fish. She often told us stories about the little stream down the hill from the house where she was born.

It had a variety of fish and small eels in it. When my brother Albert was about 12 years old, he became adept at catching fish for the family table. I liked to go with him. My job was to pick up the ones he threw on the bank and put them in a small sack. He used a three-pronged spear that he made himself. One day when I was about six years old, I took a knife from the kitchen with me to the little stream because I wanted to catch a fish the way Albert did with his spear. There were so many small fish that they swam around my feet in the clear water. I thought it would be so easy to do. I waited for the right moment and thrust the knife down into the water. Suddenly, I felt pain and saw the water go red. It took a moment for me to realize that I had stabbed myself in the foot!

I waved my foot in the water thinking I would wash off the blood. But the red cloud just got bigger, so I finally climbed out. When Albert saw my injury, he wrapped my foot in a handkerchief and told me to go home and show it to Mother. For some reason, I hid in the cellar instead. By the time my mother found me, I had lost a lot of blood. I had sliced the two veins across the top of my foot. My mother carried me into the house and bandaged my foot and kept asking, "Mimans (a childhood nickname), what were you thinking? Why were you hiding?" I got special soups and lots of rest for several days and then I was back to my usual activities, but I never tried to spear any fish again.

Max assured Momma that he would use only fishing poles and spinners to catch fish just the way Papa did. I must admit that I tended to tune out his extensive chatter about fish and fishing implements. Max and Papa would have long discussions about the best spinners and fishing methods. Their mutual interest drew them close, while Andrit was not interested in touching a fish with the proverbial ten-foot pole. My only interest was eating them after Momma fried them in butter and picked out the bones.

Ernina was not going to visit us that summer, but she did call us on the phone. Our phone, a party line, wasn't easy to get through. But if you had an important call, you could ask whoever was talking if you could use the phone. Ernina did not have her own phone, but was able to use a neighbor's on rare occasions. Mostly Momma communicated with her by letter. I didn't know it then, but Momma hoped to travel to Canada the next summer to visit her.

Jurit always had jobs so he was gone most of the summer days. He and Andrit lived in the little house year round, since the main house was too small for all of us. Many years later, he confessed that on weekend nights, Andrit would help him push his car out of the yard on to Spring Road which sloped if you turned left. He wouldn't start the car until he was well down the hill. By the time he came home, every one was sound asleep and no one heard him pull up by the barn. Living in the little house was ideal for him since he could go to all the polka dances—the parents never knew because Andrit never told anyone.

Andrit liked to read and draw. He had a talent for drawing and spent a lot of time in the little house drawing and reading. He also spent more time in the kitchen than any of the other kids and learned to bake bread and make cookies and generally help with meal preparation. Everyone else, including Momma, preferred to be outside in the summer, but Andrit was content to putter around inside. Although he would help with outside chores, they never seemed to interest him.

Papa took his two-week vacation to bring in the hay crop and otherwise work around the yard and the house. When the fresh hay was in the mow, we were allowed to sleep out there instead of in the house. The fragrance was wonderful, but the scratchy hay and the wild chirping of birds at first light caused me to rethink that particular adventure.

During the last days of August, the goldenrod flowers turned brown and transformed into seeds. Their pungent scent wafted over the pasture and from the roadside ditches and the edges of the fields. They were not fussy about where they grew and the cows would not eat them, so they multiplied in peace. That scent is forever associated in my mind with fall and the return to school.

My parents and the bigger brothers had many tasks involving harvesting the garden, picking apples from the many trees around the yard, and putting away machinery for the winter. I put my "horse collection" up in the barn in a section that had boards and other odds and ends. I don't remember if I ever took them down again. I was excited to go back to school and that was what preoccupied me.

The previous year I had started to spend some time chatting with the only other girl in my class. She had called me on the phone during the summer. All I wanted to talk about was cows, but she admitted she never went into their barn if she could help it. We didn't have much in common, but I liked the idea of expanding my social network.

Second grade was much like first grade, but more comfortable since I now knew the ropes and the players. My only continuing difficulty was getting enough books. Sometime that winter, Andrit learned about the public library in Wausau, so whenever Momma went to town on a weekend, he and I went along. After gathering the limit of four books (Andrit had helped me find them in the teenage section) and taking them to the check-out desk, the librarian said, "No, no, little girl, those are not for you." She directed me to the children's section instead. I had already looked through them and had found nothing of interest since those books were far too simple for my reading level.

Having learned that there are ways around rigid authority figures and desperate to take home the books I had collected, I took them to Momma. I asked her to check them out. She asked me what they were. "Animal stories," I said. She took them to the desk. When the librarian glared in my direction, I was quite busy studying the floor and the windows. I can still see her angry look while she snapped open the covers and smashed the date stamp on the little card that went into the back pocket. I don't know how I knew that it was not a good idea to gloat at the angry librarian. I did not meet her glance and assumed as angelic a pose as any eight-year-old could muster. I also knew instinctively that it was wrong of her to deny me access to more challenging books.

That winter I had colds and respiratory ailments, sometimes with a cough. Momma, looking worried, called the doctor who made house calls. He usually gave me an antibiotic shot in the butt and told her to give me lots of fluids. I also got Ritz crackers and ginger ale, and Momma sat and read stories to me. She had read the *White Book of Latvian Folktales* to us before, but I had her read it again from the beginning. I looked at it on my own when she was busy. In that way, I started to learn to read Latvian. Since there are no silent letters in the Latvian language, it is actually much easier to learn than English. Overall, being sick did not seem like such a bad thing to me.

Over the previous year, we had met several Latvian families who lived in the area. Once a month, after the Latvian church service, there was a potluck lunch at someone's house. Momma often made her torte to take along. Most of the families had farms, although the husbands often worked in factories as well. The wives were the ones who managed the dairy herds and did most of the daily milking and feeding of the cattle.

I spent most of the visits in the barns or near the outside pens looking at whatever livestock was available. Momma soon learned to bring along other clothes and shoes for me to change into after the church service, since the areas I liked to explore often had animal droppings. We would also get together with the other families for birthday celebrations and similar events. When the gatherings were at our house I had to help put out dishes and silverware.

Sometimes our parents went to evening social events and left us at home with Jurit or Andrit in charge. Jurit would usually organize outside games involving softball or volley ball or badminton. Andrit would read stories to us and sometimes they were scary ones like Edgar Alan Poe's "The Cask of Amontillado." I never liked being scared, but since I did not want to go to bed while anything was going on I stayed and listened. I much preferred stories about animals, but even *Black Beauty,* which turned out okay in the end, caused me a lot of stress to read.

My single-minded interest in cows was noted by the family and for the previous several Christmases I had gotten small rubber cattle, my favorite toys. That spring I found a solid wood box about a foot square with very low sides which I appropriated. I arranged hay and asked Momma for something small that would hold water. She gave me a small measuring cup made of tin. It was the right size, but the handle took up room so I took it to Jurit who cut off the handle with a pair of tin snips. My family had gotten used to my projects and rarely asked, "What do you want that for?" or "What are you making?" I was all set so I put all my favorite cows into my box. Whenever we went visiting, I would take my little "cow world" along.

Sometime that early summer of my eighth year, I learned that we were going to travel to Canada to visit Aunt Ernina. Jurit would do all the driving in the new family car! Papa would stay home and use Jurit's car to go to work. He would also take care of the animals and the garden while we were gone.

When the trunk was packed with our clothes, I tucked *cow world* into a corner under other things so I was all set. Early one morning we headed north and drove up to Upper Michigan and crossed into Canada over the long bridge that connects the two countries. We had to stop at Customs on the other side, but got through that okay and then headed east. I don't think we stopped at any motels just parked here and there so that Jurit could sleep for a while. The three of us kids were tangled in sleep in the back seat. Later Momma sat with us so that Andrit would have more room to sleep in the front. Sometime the next day we got to Montreal and found Ernina's apartment.

She was very excited to see us and had set the table with all kinds of food and had made beds for us around her apartment. I think we all crashed and took long naps. Ernina had taken her vacation so that she could spend time with us and show us the sights of Montreal. The two sisters would talk late into the evening about the homeland and the relatives. I busied myself with my cows. I don't know what the boys did, but I think Jurit took Momma and Ernina for more extended tours of the city.

Because Momma and Ernina enjoyed each other's company a great deal, I asked Ernin why she couldn't move to America to live with us. She said she didn't drive and needed to be able to take a bus to work. She also said she really did not want to live out in the country the way we did.

She gave me a present made by a friend at her request. It was an artistic carving of a rearing horse (I did not appreciate it until I was much older). I did understand though that Ernin loved me and had such a special thing made for me. It would be 15 years before I saw Montreal again when I came to spend a summer with her. I saw the city through an adult's eyes and came to understand why she had never been willing to move away.

After about two weeks with Ernina, we headed south back to America and stopped off in Connecticut where Momma's cousin Anna lived with her family. We spent a few days with them and then headed home. Papa was very happy to see us and glad to have help with all the farm animals and other work that needed to be done. We were all glad to be home where we could sleep in our own beds.

Third Grade Among the Pines

Although I had been expecting another fine year at Liberty School, we were all surprised to learn that the Country Schools were being closed down; Liberty was among the first to go. We would have to travel to Mosinee to the elementary school, becoming part of a much larger student body. I don't know how Max and Andrit felt, but I thought there would probably be more books in a bigger school.

There were lots of kids as well. The days were never dull. I spent time getting to know my classmates and finding more books to read. Every grade had its own teacher and our class had about 20 third-graders. We had a separate teacher for art and another one for music. The school had large windows and was set among old pine trees. At recess time, the teacher opened windows and let fresh, pine-scented air fill the room.

A large play area surrounded the three-story building, which had makeshift softball fields and running-around room. A basketball court was at either end of the school. I watched boys playing with the round brown ball with some interest since I had never seen anyone play basketball before. Max soon learned about the several paved circles in the yard and explained the rules for playing marbles. The object was to knock your opponent's marble outside the circle while your marble stayed in. If I remember right, special shooters, larger than regular marbles, were immune to confiscation. But if you lost, you had to give up other marbles. I don't know where he got the first few that he started out with, but pretty soon Max was a marble shark. He brought home more and more of them. He let me pick out a few (I chose them for their iridescent colors) which I carried around in my pocket.

My teacher was a young woman who left after a couple months because she had a baby. Her replacement was Mr. Marco. I sat in the back because I had gotten accustomed to paying limited attention to what the rest of the class was doing (I was reading books and drawing pictures).

When Mr. Marco noticed some of my cow pictures, he gave me a few lessons in shading and perspective. He seemed to lose interest when no matter how the picture started it always ended up with cows in it. Because he insisted on class participation, I had to listen more closely so that I could answer questions that came my way. None of it was hard though. I had read the textbook in the first few weeks of school and completed the work books way ahead. Mr. Marco told me not to do that, but to stay with the class.

I would put the book I was interested in reading in my desk, prop up the lid just enough so that I could read it, and turn the pages surreptitiously. I learned to hide books inside my coat and smuggle them outside. I would sit on some rocks, screened by small trees, and read during recess and lunch hour. I watched other girls play hopscotch and jump rope, but I could not get interested in those activities. Playground time was much different from what it had been at Liberty School. Boys and girls played separately and the grades also were segregated. The old camaraderie of the basement games at Liberty School was gone.

After school and on weekends, Duksit and Max were my companions. Sometime that fall, Papa found Mintz (an older cat when we got him) dead in the drive-through area of the barn. He did not appear to have been injured; we never knew what caused him to sicken and die. Momma would put down an old pan with milk in it for the other cats hanging around from time to time. They came and went and were half wild, but they helped keep the rodent population in check.

One fall day I had an inspiration. I called Duksit in to the porch where I had brought one of my older flannel shirts. I put one of his paws in one sleeve and stretched the shirt over his back in order to try to fit the other paw in. It was tight and my plan was not going too well. When Duksit growled at me, I was not deterred. I kept trying to stuff his other paw into the sleeve. All of a sudden he growled again and then nipped me in the chest. I dropped the shirt and ran into the house to find Momma. I whimpered to her that Duksit had bitten me. Her first words were, "What did *you* do to the dog?"

I started formulating my defense as I followed her to the porch. She saw the problem immediately and took the shirt off his back, removed his paw, and told me it was much too small a shirt for my project. She opened the porch door and Duksit bolted. Momma looked at my injury where he had barely broken my skin, put some iodine on it, and told me to go play outside. Duksit found me almost immediately and licked my hand. I told him it was okay. After that incident, I only put hats and sunglasses on him. He was very patient with my need to change his appearance.

Momma often said that she wished that she had learned to play the piano when she was young. That fall, the parents bought an upright with a nice sound. Max and I, and later Andrit, started taking lessons. We had a variety of teachers and over the next eight years I learned enough to entertain myself. A music teacher at the high school who gave us lessons for a while said that I liked to play by ear and not concentrate on playing the exact notes. He was right. But the lessons helped expose me to the wonderful world of classical music. I still play from time to time and still enjoy myself while I am doing it.

That Christmas Ernina sent me a beautiful ceramic horse. When I look at it now I realize that whoever made it was very familiar with horses because its expression shows such depth and individuality. This was the start of my ceramic horse collection and survived hours and hours of play. Eventually it suffered a broken leg, but I fixed that with glue. Whenever I see it on my kitchen shelf, I think about Ernina. Sometimes I also think that I probably never told her how much she meant to me.

For my ninth birthday in January, I got a book, *Justin Morgan Had a Horse*, from my parents as a present. I actually think that Andrit picked it out. When I read it in a day, Momma was disappointed. She said, "Who can possibly buy enough books if you are going to read them so fast!" I thought that over but never thought a day would come when I could acquire more books than I could read.

Spring in Wisconsin arrived later than in South Dakota, but when it came, it brought a rush of soft colors and blossoms and filled the air with the scent of new life. The ditches ran with little streams. Max even found a place on the farm that had a spring and a little creek. He spent a lot of time clearing its route of debris, but also placing stones here and there to make it more interesting. He made a small dam to create a pool and then more dams to create more pools. He was quite disappointed that everything dried up in a few weeks when the spring melt was over.

One weekend day in early summer, I woke up to learn that I would have to accompany Papa and Parsla on an expedition. We were going to see a farmer with a bull. The purpose of the trip was a mystery to me, but Papa insisted that I come along because Parsla always behaved better when I was around. He put a halter on her and held the lead while I got a small willow branch switch just in case I needed it.

We headed down the hill and turned left on Maple Ridge Road. Years later I realized that it was a two-mile hike to that farm, but that morning it did not seem very far. Parsla would stop at every opportunity and start to graze along the side of the road. She would not move again until I tapped her on the hip. Then she would stomp along for a while swinging her tail back and forth vigorously. I knew she was annoyed because there was knee-high grass and red clover everywhere and she was not getting a chance to eat it.

When we arrived at our destination, Papa talked to the farmer and then told me to stand behind a solid board fence and stay there until he came back. He took Parsla with him. I moved down the fence until I came to a spot where a knot had fallen out and left a hole so I looked through it. The farmer reappeared with a bull whom he led with a rope tied to a ring in his nose. After some sniffing and snorting, the bull jumped on Parsla's back and a moment later lowered himself down again. The farmer led him around in a circle for a while and then the bull did it again.

I quickly went back to the spot where I was supposed to be waiting and thought over what I had seen. It still did not make any sense to me, but it was clear that a physical connection was established between the two animals. I did not let on to Papa that I had been watching and did not ask him any questions on the way home.

Some time later I told Max about what I had seen. My theory was that this sort of activity was necessary between male and female animals in order to produce baby animals. The details of just how that worked I did not know. Max was appalled and would not have any of it. He said that babies came from God. I asked him, "Well, then, why would the bull jump on Parsla's back?" He said that was a signal to God that he should send a baby calf. I did not accept Max's view, but my own theory needed further development, so I let it go.

The Family History

Most of the family stories were told in bits and pieces over many years until eventually I thought I had the complete account—or at least as much as the parents were going to tell. They took the position that they were entitled to some privacy regarding their personal histories. I took the position that once you had children, your life story belonged to the family. Our differing viewpoints made my mission of gleaning the family stories more difficult. I learned early, however, that parents can be worn down by repeated questioning.

By the time I started fourth grade, I knew that we were different from most of the people who lived around us and most of the kids in my school. Until high school, when a foreign-exchange student showed up, we were the only foreigners in the school. I started to question the parents individually and together about where we came from and why we left the homeland.

I wanted to know how they met (asking them about happier times would get them talking more readily). My parents met on a ski train. Or at least my father saw my mother and was startled by the immediate thought that she was going to be the one he would marry. It was a day trip for students and young adults that left Riga, Latvia, early in the morning and traveled to the largest hill in the area, where cross-country and downhill skiing was possible. At a cabin on the hill, local farmers sold fresh bread, honey, and hot tea to hungry skiers who gathered there after hours out in the cold air.

On the way home, they sat in the railroad car that provided music and had room for dancing. My father remembered dancing with Momma. Although she remembered taking several of those skiing trips, she had no memory of Papa being among the passengers!

They met again in Riga when she was a university student and he was the chemistry instructor who set up experiments and supervised students in her botany lab classes. Orphaned by the age of seven, Papa had worked very hard to get through school and was hoping to earn the Latvian equivalent of a PhD and become a professor at that same university. He was interested in how soil and water quality could be improved to help the average farmer.

In the fall of 1938, they were married, when Momma was 23 and Papa was 28. They lived in Riga where the following June, Jurit was born. Momma said it was such a hopeful time for them. Latvia had been free for 20 years and many positive changes had taken place in that time. Everyone thought that the future could only be better. Momma remembered walking down their street with infant Jurit in her arms. The chestnut trees were in bloom, their fragrance filled the air, and their white candlestick blossoms dropped a carpet of petals that whirled around her feet as she walked. Momma said everything changed when the War started that fall. Momma always said that war was a terrible thing; they both got sad expressions when they thought about it. They said that those stories would have to wait until I was older.

Sometimes when Momma was in a pensive mood, she would talk about the past. One summer day we were alone at home (I can't remember how old I was but I would guess between 10 and 11) when she started talking about her parents and how they happened to get married. She often said that her father did not enjoy living on the farm or doing farm work and that he was very sociable, but that her mother was shy and loved the quiet solitude of farm life. Momma told this story about her parents:

My mother had been in love with someone else before she met my father. When she started grade school, she was about eight years old (kids had to be able to walk to school, so they usually started school later). She was very uncomfortable and did not look at any one. She just looked down at her desk and did not make eye contact with anyone. An older boy came up to her and gently pushed her head back so that he could see her face and told her that his name was Peter. He asked her her name; she told him it was Berta. From that day on they were friends. In the spring, he picked tiny violets and gave her a bouquet when she arrived at school.

He walked with her and kept her company. He was quiet and thoughtful. Because he was of a slight build and generally did not have a strong constitution, his parents encouraged him to study to be a teacher. They remained close friends and Grandmother thought they would grow up to be married. Because Latvia did not have any universities of its own in the late 1800s, he would have to go to St. Petersburg in Russia to go to college. Before he left he asked her to promise that she would wait for him. She said she would.

They wrote regularly and he reported about life in the big city and how his studies were going. She wrote about life on the farm with her parents, Mr. and Mrs. Rutkis, her sisters, and a brother who also lived there. Then his letters stopped. She kept writing and asking what was wrong and why wasn't he writing. There was no reply. Eventually, she stopped writing and decided that he must have met someone else. At that time, engagements were not made public until a wedding was planned. There was no one she could ask about his plans because girls did not make such inquiries in those times. She was heartbroken.

Around that time she met my grandfather, Andrejs Kalnins. Tall and blond and smitten by her, he kept after her until she agreed to marry him. She was still so sad that she didn't much care what she did or where she would live. In 1903, when Berta was 21 and Andrejs about five years older, they got married. The revolt of '05 destroyed the telegraph lines and caused him to lose his employment. In 1906 they had their first child, Arvids. So they moved to the Inn and Tavern where Grandfather tried to make a go of being a tavern keeper, but ended up having to farm. This is where they raised their seven children.

After they had moved and on a visit home, Grandmother learned a terrible thing. A man who worked at the Post Office in her home town and who had been pursuing her and trying to get her to marry him while Peter was away at college was telling a shocking story in the local bars. He would get drunk and say that since Berta would not marry him, he had decided to make sure she didn't marry Peter either.

He had watched for Peter's letters and destroyed them. He did the same with Berta's letters to Peter. He noted with satisfaction when the letters stopped coming. Now he thought he would be able to win her over, but much to his chagrin, she up and married Andrejs and moved away. My mother was crushed. She had just assumed that Peter did not love her anymore and did not want to marry her.

I almost held my breath as Momma told this story and did not want her to be interrupted. Although at that time I really did not understand much about jealousy and lost love, I did feel how mean that mailman must have been. I had to know whether they ever saw each other again. Momma said when her mother was pregnant and had gone to her own mother's funeral in the spring of 1915, Peter was there.

He sought her out and they had a long talk about what had happened. He told her he still loved her and wanted her to come away with him. She said, "But I have four children and a fifth on the way." He said, "It doesn't matter; bring them, too." But she said that so many things had changed and her husband Andrejs was not at fault for how their lives had turned out. She said she couldn't abandon their home while Andrejs was away in the War and that he should find someone else to marry.

Every time I had Momma tell me the story I felt sad at how Grandmother's life had turned out because of the selfish Post Office worker. When I was much older, I asked Momma how her mother felt about how those events changed the course of her life. Grandmother's attitude was that God knew what was best for her even when she couldn't understand why things turned out the way they did. She said that Peter's father died of TB and that Peter also suffered from that disease and died young. He did marry, but she did not know if he had any children. Grandmother said it would be a terrible thing to have sickly children. She said she knew that her strong healthy children were a blessing.

One day it also dawned on me that if Grandmother had married Peter the course of the family history would have changed considerably, and I wouldn't even be here! I filched a piece of cake and went outside and found a quiet place to eat it and mull things over. Years later, when I spent a summer in Montreal with Aunt Erna, I asked her whether she had heard that story. She said she hadn't, but as the oldest girl who was five years older than Momma, she had moved away to find work in the city. She also said, "Our mother talked to little Olga a lot—she was always a good listener."

That fall school was underway when a teacher tapped me to become a safety patrol member. As a member of the safety patrol, I received a belt with a section that went over the shoulder to which a badge was attached. Each safety patrol person carried a pole with a flag that said "Safety Patrol." Members guarded the crosswalks where the younger children crossed the street either in the morning or at lunch time. Adults patrolled the area at the end of the day when the buses arrived to take the country kids home. I was diligent and reliable. The reward was a trip to Wisconsin Dells at the end of the school year. That trip was the first time that I had gone away overnight without the family.

Another privilege that started that year was that fourth-graders and older kids were allowed to walk the two blocks downtown over the lunch hour. Usually that meant a trip to the candy store, where, for a quarter, you could buy quite a bit of candy. I would snack on my purchases all afternoon. By the end of the day my cache was gone, but the craving for sweets was not. I did not get an allowance, but did get small amounts of money for a birthday. If I asked for some money, Momma always wanted to know what it was for. I knew I couldn't tell her that it was for candy because she did not approve of too many sweets and told us sweets were bad for our teeth.

Having accompanied my mother on many shopping trips, I knew that she always had change, and I knew where she kept it. I told myself that I was only borrowing the small amounts that I pilfered from her purse and that I would pay it back later when I was older. I never got caught, but the dependence on sugar certainly did not do me any good.

During the winter of that year, we were required to go outside during our lunch break and recess. I started to notice the behavior of an older boy in seventh grade that I had not encountered before. Usually the older kids hung around one end of the building and the smaller ones at the other. But this boy would wander all around and he would usually have two or three pals who obviously looked up to him. One of his favorite activities was to push the smaller boys into snow drifts or put snow down the backs of their shirts or smear their faces with it. He also liked to trip them from behind. He would be careful to go on the attack only when the teacher was not around.

On one occasion I intervened when his bullying seemed extreme. I told him to go and pick on someone his own size. He sneered at me, but left the area. I asked the boys he had been picking on why they did not tell a teacher. They said the bully's father was important in the community and that nothing would be done to him. He would just get meaner.

Some weeks later I had just come outside at lunch time to the concrete area at our end of the building. The snow was deep and the only open spaces were the concrete walks and the basketball court at either end of the building. He was there again making fun of the little kids and pushing them around. His cohorts would laugh loudly at whatever he did. All of a sudden he went up behind a small boy and tripped him and gave him a vicious shove. The boy fell hard and ripped his jeans at both knees. He started crying as he looked at his torn pants. The bully and his pals were laughing. I felt a cold rage that I had never felt before.

I looked around and saw the snow piles behind where the bully was standing. I ran up the snow pile and jumped on his back and pulled him down backwards. He was on his knees with my arm locked around his neck and I used my other hand to tighten the hold. I choked him with all my might and talked in his ear at the same time. I told him to leave our end of the building and never come back and to never pick on the little kids again. His face was a bright red. I knew I was impacting his breathing. When he croaked out an "okay" to my terms, I let him go.

He got up and ran away. I never saw him again. I am sure that having a girl get the best of him was mortifying. He must have gone home for lunch from then on. The next year when the new high school was finished, the seventh-and eighth-graders moved to the old high school and did not mingle with the lower grades. I often thought over this incident. I had never felt the need to intervene when the small boys fought with each other even though sometimes they were quite mean about it and caused injuries. I was also a little frightened by the intensity of my emotions when confronted by what I saw as unfair behavior. In the future, I found other ways to deal with such situations, as I never felt good about the violence I had resorted to.

My Sister Laura

Although she lived only a short time, she impacted our family in many ways. When I was quite small, I wondered what my life would be like with an older sister. I imagined that she would be an ally and take my side whenever dealing with the brothers got to be too much for me. I decided that she would like to hang out and chat and would probably like animals as much as I did. Later, I thought we would discuss books that we were reading.

Bringing up Laura's name reminded my parents of the War and the upheaval the War had caused in their lives, so it was a subject that had to be approached carefully. But my curiosity about my missing sibling caused me to gently prod them for information. What they told me about her and that period of time came in bits and pieces, over many years, and culminated when my mother showed me a diary. She had kept this diary from the time the family arrived in Germany in the fall of 1944; it ended on the day that Laura died, March 19, 1945.

My mother had forgotten that she even had it or what it said. She showed me a lock of blond hair that had grown stiff and dry with the passage of years. She had cut it from Laura's head after she died. She told me about the elderly German women who had come up to them in the park near where they first lived when they went to Berlin. Obviously they had very little to eat themselves, yet they gave her a handful of fruit (this happened more than once) "for the little girl." Even after more than 50 years, Momma cried remembering the kindness of strangers.

The diary revealed that Laura had one respiratory ailment after another accompanied by regular bouts of fever which got worse and more frequent when they had to move from the suburbs to a several story apartment building closer to the center of the city. When she was feeling better, Laura would ask Momma to play "Let's Visit Mimite." In the game, Momma would knock on an imaginary door. Laura, having covered her head with a scarf, would be Mimite. She would pretend to open the door. She would hug and kiss Momma and tell her how glad she was that they had come home and could all be together again. As I read the diary, I marveled how a two-and-a-half-year-old could come up with a game that was a comfort to her but also an attempt to comfort Momma (who missed her mother, Mimite terribly).

Momma noted that five-year-old Jurit was always willing to go to the store for her. He would clutch the ration card in one hand, while turning his other arm as if he were an airplane, and run down the street. Papa was at work and Momma had to depend on Jurit since Laura was often sick. Momma was also pregnant, and climbing up and down all the stairs was very tiring.

In several places in the diary, Momma wrote that when Laura was sick, she wanted Momma to draw ducks. Always ducks, nothing else. I asked Momma if she knew why Laura was so interested in ducks. When they first arrived in Berlin, Momma told me, they had lived in the suburbs. There was a lovely park nearby, with a pond, where they went almost every day. They would take crusts of bread to feed the ducks. Laura loved feeding the ducks.

When they moved closer to the city center there was no park nearby. They were living in the apartment building in the late winter of 1945 when the Allies mounted an intensive carpet bombing of residential areas of Berlin. The intention was to break the will of the German Resistance and put an end to the War. The residents, however, had no idea why their area was targeted. Night after night bombers flew over their apartment building, the air raid sirens sounded, signaling everyone to run to the basement. Dust drizzled from the basement ceiling, and the huddled residents could hear and feel the thud of the bombs falling.

As small, frightened children cried, everyone held their breath thinking this night would be their last. In the morning, when they went outside, they would see the buildings up and down their street that had collapsed. Momma said she can still hear the sound of people calling for help. There was no heavy machinery to clear away the debris, and there was no help. The neighborhood housed mostly women, children, and old people. After a while the calls for help faded away. The living faced another night of dread.

When the bombing grew more intense Papa found out about an underground bunker that would shelter children only. They started taking the children there at night. Papa thought that if they were killed maybe the little ones would survive. Momma often said when the subject of the War came up that they should not have taken Jurit and Laura to the bunker because she believed that was where Laura caught the virus that killed her—probably diphtheria. Although our parents took her to a hospital she died. Momma said it happened so fast. Momma said they should have relied on God and stayed where they were. Papa's face crumpled as he said that he made the best decision he could at the time.

After I read the diary, I reminded Momma that Laura was sickly the entire time they were in Germany and would have been vulnerable to whatever was going around. I also reminded her that it was a miracle that any of them survived; so many small children in Europe did not. I think that my parents never got over feeling bad about Laura's death. After I read the diary, I realized how young my parents were, the difficult decisions they had to make, and how their choices affected the family's future.

Although the War in Europe started in 1939, Latvia did not feel its effects until Russia occupied the Baltic States in 1940. During the next year, Russia rounded up more than 40,000 Latvians, loaded them into cattle cars, and shipped them to Siberia. Most of them were never heard from again.

When the Germans advanced in 1941 and pushed the Russians out, Papa said that everyone was happy believing that the Germans had come to liberate them. It did not take long to realize that another form of terror was replacing the familiar one. Anyone who talked about a free Latvia disappeared in the night. The oppression of the Jewish population became evident. Papa said that late at night he and Momma talked in whispers about their hopes that the War would be over soon and that life in Latvia would return to normal. Every day was overcast with dread and fear of not knowing what might happen next.

In the spring of 1944, when Papa was 33 years old and working at the University of Latvia, he was drafted by the occupying German forces. The German SS was gathering up scientists. Some of Papa's colleagues refused to respond and took off into the forests to join the Latvian resistance. But soon it became clear that the *families* of the men who refused the order to report for the draft disappeared in the night, never to be seen again. Papa said that he thought about Momma and his two small children. Laura was not even two years old and Jurit was four. He did not know what to do, but decided that he could not abandon them. He did not know what the Nazis were going to try to make him do. Maybe he was just putting off the inevitable, but for now he would respond to the draft notice.

On one of the many occasions when I made him tell this story, he said, "You know, Inite, there may come a time in your life where the choices you have seem equally terrible and the only thing you can do is to take the next possible step and then see what happens."

With fear in his heart, he went to basic training. In the six-weeks training period, he learned how to fire a rifle and received a uniform and identity papers. When he went back to work, it was not at the University, but at a facility in Riga managed by the German Army. His job was still in his field, water quality. Now he worked on developing water purification kits for soldiers and field tests so that soldiers could determine whether wells were poisoned. He was much relieved that nothing more was demanded of him. The relief was short lived. In September of 1944 when the Germans started losing ground to the Russians, who were advancing from the east, he became fearful again. Papa said he was convinced that if the Russians caught him, they would shoot him on sight. They would not care why he was in a German uniform or what he had been doing. Even if he ditched his uniform, he feared someone would turn him in for having cooperated with the Germans.

He told Momma that she could stay in Riga with the children, but he didn't think he had any other alternative. Momma decided that she, too, must leave and reassured herself that the War would soon be over and they could go back to their life.

They traveled by truck out of Riga and then by train to Berlin. Papa came later along the same route and they met up in Berlin where housing had been arranged for them in a suburban household. But as the War went on, that host family had friends and relatives fleeing ahead of the Russians. They no longer had room for the Pogainis family.

One of Papa's colleague's, a German scientist, had extra rooms in an apartment he owned. The parents were glad to have somewhere to live. Because it was on the fourth floor and had no elevator, Momma depended on little five-year-old Jurit to get milk and other rationed items. Papa reported to his new workplace every day although he said not much work was being done. There were a number of scientists from other countries and German ones, too. Together, they whispered information about the progress of the War. They had to be careful because an SS officer patrolled the halls to make sure no one thought about leaving. Papa said everyone feared him. Rumors abounded that he shot people on the spot if they disobeyed his directives.

Papa would pause sometimes in the retelling of his story and point out that if he had not been a chemist with a good reputation at the University, Hitler's henchmen would probably not have been interested in him and the family would have stayed in Latvia. On the other hand, being a scientist probably saved him from death on the Eastern front. At the very end of the War, Hitler ordered every able-bodied man—boys and old men included—to be sent east to try to stop the Russians. But to the very end, Hitler would not allow "my scientists" to be expended in that way.

On March 29, 1945, Momma and Jurit boarded a train that took women and children out of Berlin. It would travel southwest as far as it could away from the

Russians. Papa, however, had to stay in Berlin. He did not know what would happen next.

After watching the train pull away (he remembered Momma's pale face in the window), he waved until all the cars were gone and then went back to their apartment. Numb and exhausted, Papa reflected on his decision to respond to the draft notice. He had hoped to save his family. Now Laura was dead. He did not know whether he would ever see Momma and Jurit again. That night there was another air raid. He stayed in bed; he did not go to the cellar. Recently a bomb had fallen in the courtyard behind the building but had not exploded. He heard the sirens, but felt too tired to move. He thought it statistically unlikely that another bomb would fall so close again. He later marveled at how extreme fatigue caused his mind to reason its way out of moving his body down to the basement.

He continued to report to his laboratory, but all that he remembered about those last days were discussions about where the American and British lines were. They all understood that their only hope was to reach one of them and surrender, because the Russians were not taking prisoners.

A few days after Momma left, Papa got a letter from her posted in Eisenach, a small town southwest of Berlin. Momma said that the train tracks went no further (they had been bombed and destroyed) and they had gotten off there. That was the last piece of mail he got from her before Berlin collapsed.

Just as he was planning how to make a run for it, the same feared SS officer came up to him, gave him a handgun, and ordered him to come outside. He had a mission for him. When they got outside, he saw a small group of young boys and old men armed with a hodgepodge of weapons, including what he thought were old hunting rifles. The officer shouted at him to lead this group and find a certain bridge over a river that was one of the routes into the city. He said that this would be Papa's last order and that he must hold that bridge to the last man.

Papa thought, "This is a suicidal mission." He did not doubt that the half-crazed SS officer would shoot him if he refused. To give himself time to think, Papa motioned for the group to follow him and set off. He knew generally where the bridge was. Although he thought about going around a corner and taking off, he did not know who his "troops" were. Maybe one of them was a fanatic Nazi and would shoot him in the back.

They kept going as fast as they could, but it took a lot longer than it would have ordinarily taken. With all the collapsed buildings and blocked streets, they had to take a circuitous route. As they moved further east, the air was filled with choking smoke and the sound of shells whistling overhead and thudding to the ground. Papa said that if he died and went to hell, he would already know what it looked like.

When they got closer to their destination, they could hear the rattling and crunching of heavy vehicles over rubble. He took one of the boys and they crawled up a pile of bricks and other debris and peeked over the top. What he saw was a relief to Papa. The bridge had already been taken. Russian tanks and armored vehicles were moving rapidly one after another into Berlin!

After they climbed back down to the others, Papa told them what he had seen. "There is no point to our mission unless we want to commit suicide," Papa said. He watched their faces as he told them they were free to go. They scattered like rabbits. He wished he had known their true feelings earlier.

He ripped off all the insignia that identified any connection with the German Army. The uniform he wore was the only clothing he had and he knew that just removing the insignia was not much of a disguise. He threw his pistol over a pile of rubble and headed back the way he had come. When I asked why he didn't keep the pistol to protect himself, he said, "I knew I could not shoot another human being even to save my own life."

The next several hours were a blur of running and climbing over rubble, running some more, always heading west, only west. Late in the day, he came to a large river he knew he must cross in order to reach the allied lines. As he looked up and down, he saw that the bridges had been destroyed and had collapsed into the water. He sat down in some tall grass to rest when he heard a sound that caused his heart to turn over.

He heard the squawking of poultry and the voices of Russian soldiers calling to one another as they chased their lunch. Papa said he flattened himself to the ground and prayed that they wouldn't find him or if they did that he would know what to say to them so that they wouldn't shoot him. They kept coming closer. He stopped breathing and closed his eyes. When it seemed that they would step on him, they caught the bird they were after. Their steps and voices receded.

Drenched in sweat and so tired that he couldn't move he lay where he was. After a while, he crawled closer to the river into some brush and settled down. He made himself as small as he could and wondered what would become of him.

Light was fading and soon it would be dark. Although he was a good swimmer, he knew the water was too cold and the river too broad to be able to swim across it. Half dozing, he wondered what he should do, but he was too tired and too afraid to leave his small lair. A voice calling from the river jolted him awake. He looked out through the branches and saw a German Army officer in a small two-man rubber raft rowing along the shore. He was calling out for any soldiers that might be hiding in the bushes. Papa tumbled down the slope in his hurry to respond.

To his amazement, at least a dozen German soldiers appeared as if out of nowhere. They had all been so quiet that they did not know that the others were there. The officer asked whether any of them knew how to handle such a small boat. Papa looked around; no one was responding so he raised his hand; he said that he knew how to do it. (He had spent many summer vacations fishing on Latvia's numerous lakes and rivers and had bought such a boat to make his expeditions easier).

The officer rowed up against the shore and told Papa to get in. He explained his plan. The two of them would row over to the other side; he would get out; then Papa would come back and pick up someone else; when they got back to the western shore, Papa would get out. The man left in the boat would go back to pick up someone else and so on until every one was across the river.

Papa said when they got across he had a strong urge to bolt and run but then thought he did not know who those soldiers were or what they may or may have done in the War. He was not going to be the one to judge them. So he rowed back, picked up another man, and when they got to the western side, he jumped out of the boat into shallow water and ran up the slope. Whether the chain continued or not, he did not know; he had done his part.

With the energy that hope brings, Papa said he walked all night and met up with German soldiers who were heading the same way. Mid-morning of the next day, they decided to sit down in the ditch and rest. Thirst had dried up his throat and he could barely speak. He couldn't remember the last time he had eaten anything.

All of a sudden a jeep with two British soldiers pulled up next to them on the road. One of the soldiers stood up in the vehicle and looked at them over the windshield. He asked whether any of them spoke English. Papa looked around and since no one volunteered, he stood up and said, "I do." The British soldier said, "Good," and threw him a canteen of water, telling him to pass it around to the others as well. He then said, "Keep walking down this road and when you meet the main force, surrender, and you will be looked after." Papa said, "Thank you"; they would do as they were told.

Papa liked to pause at this point in his story and stress this point: "It is important to learn anything and everything you can because you never know when it might come in handy." He pointed out that since he went to school in Russia during the First World War, he had learned Russian so he might have been able to reason with the Russian soldiers had they caught him, but he always added, "I'm glad that I never had to find out!"

He also said that learning to handle a small rubber raft allowed him to be the first person in that chain, and it might have saved him as well. Then knowing English (he was fluent in several languages) helped him to understand the rules in the Prisoner of War camp. He was able to explain things to others who had been detained. Later his knowledge of languages allowed him to work for the American Army as an interpreter.

When they reached the main British lines, they were put on trucks and moved north and west to a Prisoner of War camp. The trip was a blur of crowding and jostling and trying to sleep sitting up. At the camp, everyone was processed, given a new identity card, and directed to where they would be sleeping. By then Papa had met up with a small group of other Latvians. They hung back as the larger group of German prisoners rushed into the building and claimed the available bunks.

It was clear that there weren't enough bunks, so Papa's group was given fresh lumber and tools to build their own. They also got new sacks filled with fresh straw and clean blankets. It was over the next few days when they realized that their bedding was free of lice and bedbugs, while the folks who had claimed the other beds were struggling with that aggravation. Papa said, "Pushing to the head of the line does not always pay off."

The British were very orderly and everyone took regular showers and had water and wash tubs available so that they could wash their clothes. Every prisoner had a job to do: sweeping the floor, dealing with garbage, or helping to distribute food. Soon after they arrived, the Red Cross distributed packages containing chocolate and cigarettes. Since Papa never smoked, he swapped his cigarettes for more chocolates or any other food he could get.

He said the British mistreated no one; the worst thing was not knowing what would happen to him. Worse still was not knowing where Momma and Jurit were. He did know that by then Momma should have had another baby and he wondered whether he would ever see any of them again.

It was in that camp that a young American soldier befriended him. Surprised that Papa spoke English, the soldier would talk with him when they encountered each other during the day. He told Papa that he longed to return home to see his family again. Papa told him about wanting to find his family. One day the soldier gave Papa a tiny Bible printed in English. Papa was surprised and very grateful to have it and he would read it whenever he had a free moment. It was the only thing he had other than the clothes on his back and his only comfort while he wondered about the fate of his family. Papa read it every day, every chance he got. Although he was generally familiar with the Bible he had never read it with such care or given it so much thought. Its pages were made of delicate paper so whenever he wasn't reading it, he kept it tucked away in his shirt pocket so that it would be safe and close to him.

In October of 1945 Papa was informed that he would be moved to a new camp—a place for displaced men who did not know where their families were. He was no longer considered a prisoner. The new place, farther north near a canal, had a small town nearby, but since he had no money, there was nothing he could do there. While it was warm enough, the men bathed and washed their clothes in the canal. Soon, however, it got too cold to do that. Housed in metal Quonset hut structures, they slept on the ground. They ate their food, usually cold, straight out of cans.

The Red Cross came by from time to time and posted a list of families seeking husbands, fathers, and brothers. Individuals and small groups of men would leave as they learned where their families were. Papa checked the list every time it was updated, but Momma's name did not appear.

His only comfort continued to be his small Bible which he read as often as he could until one day an event changed that. He was sitting and reading when another Latvian man came up to him and lifted a page and rubbed it between his fingers. He said, "Your book would make really nice cigarette papers." Papa was shocked, closed the Bible, and tucked it away. Several men in his hut, desperate for cigarettes, would go into town, pick up butts, and collect the tobacco they contained. They would then have to find paper to roll new cigarettes.

Now Papa became afraid that someone would steal his little Bible while he slept. So he made a pocket inside his shirt and pinned the Bible securely in the pocket. Confident he had done a good job, he was sure no one could get at it without waking him. He also decided that it was not safe to let folks even see that he had it. Feeling it close to his heart was a comfort, but not so much as when he could read it every day.

Since he could not bathe, he was aware of the lice infesting his clothing. He worried that Momma and Jurit were still in Eisenach (he had learned that Eisenach was in the Russian section of divided Germany, so he would not be able to rejoin them). And what if they were dead? He started to think that he would have no reason to live without them.

As it got colder, Papa started to sink into a depression. He lost interest in eating the cold food and ate less and less. He also didn't feel like making the effort to get closer to the heat source to sleep at night. The Red Cross list was the only thing he looked forward to, yet time after time there was no news about Momma.

Finally, one cold night in December, he drifted off to sleep and dreamed that he was nice and warm. In his dream, little Laura came to him, looking as she had that last summer at the seashore, her hair bleached blonde. She was wearing a little white dress and had bare feet. Her skin was like honey from running around outside all summer. He felt so happy to see her. She came up to him, took his hand and tugged at him to follow her. He started to follow her when he stopped and said, "I can't go with you because I don't know where Momma and Jurit are and they may need me." He realized while dreaming that if he went with her he would die too. He started awake shivering.

He got up, moved closer to the stove, and gave himself a talking to. He had to marshal his energy; he could not give up. He didn't know where they were and until he knew that he couldn't just mope around and let himself deteriorate so badly. He could not give up hope.

Three days later, the updated list showed that Momma was in Wurzburg and that she was looking for Edmunds. Papa was beside himself with excitement because Wurzburg was in the American sector. When he asked the camp administrator how to get there, the official told him that the Red Cross would make the arrangements, which would probably take two or three weeks.

A couple other Latvians suggested that they go downtown to the train station. They knew a Latvian who worked there and they wanted to ask him for advice. He told them that a coal train that went through Wurzburg stopped there every other day on its way south. It had priority on the tracks because coal was such a necessity for everyone. He told them to climb onto one of the open coal cars, keep their heads down whenever they came to a town, and they would get to Wurzburg in a couple days. They shouldn't have any trouble.

Later that night, they walked back to the train station; they climbed into a coal car, crouching down out of sight. Soon the train started moving. Papa said December in northern Germany is very cold. The wind whipping through the open car must have been cold too, but he didn't feel it. He didn't feel hunger or thirst or cold. He was so excited and felt so relieved that he cried and then he smiled and then he cried again.

He got off in Wurzburg and since he spoke fluent German, he was able to ask several people for directions. Eventually he made his way to the displaced persons camp. He located the Latvian section and asked someone where Olga Pogainis was living. He walked down a long hall and knocked on her door.

Momma said that since it was nine o'clock at night she wondered who it could be. Jurit and eight-month-old Andrit were asleep in their cots in the one room that they all shared. She opened the door and saw a thin man covered in coal dust from head to foot. She wondered why the coal man was making a delivery so late at night. She did not recognize Papa until he smiled. It was Christmas Eve 1945.

Leaving Berlin

Momma's last entry in her diary was on March 19, 1945—the day Laura died. It read, "Laura died today and I can't feel anything." Shock and numbness continued for days afterward. She was barely able to get out of bed. Ten days later, the order came for women and children to get on trains and leave the city. She remembered watching Papa standing on the platform until she couldn't see him any more and wondering whether she would ever see him again.

Momma and Jurit had one small suitcase between them which held their few items of clothing and some baby clothes for the new member of the family she was expecting. When the train stopped in Eisenach, a small city southwest of Berlin, she did not know how far they had traveled. Everyone was ordered off the train. They could go no farther because the tracks were destroyed beyond that point. They were told to leave their possessions on the train. They could retrieve them once arrangements were made for housing. Momma had told Papa that she would send him a letter as soon as they knew where they were going to be, so she did that right away.

A minister and his family took Momma and Jurit into their house. When they went back for their suitcase, they learned that the train had been robbed by escaped forced laborers who were roaming the countryside. Now all they had was the clothes on their back and a small attic room. Momma piled some pillows around them and they fell into an exhausted sleep even though planes flew overhead, strafing the buildings.

A couple days later, Jurit awoke with a severe fever and very red skin. The minister drove them to the hospital. There they learned that Jurit had scarlet fever and would have to be quarantined for several weeks. Momma was allowed to say goodbye to him. As she looked at him, she started sobbing uncontrollably. Jurit pulled at her sleeve and said, "Don't cry, Momma, I am not going to die."

When she had calmed down somewhat, she went out to the waiting area and told the minister what was wrong. He looked dismayed and backed away from her. He said he would not be able to take her back to his house. He got into his car and drove away leaving Momma where she stood. In a daze, she did not know what to do. She was separated from every familiar person and place; she had no food and no shelter. Too tired to think, she walked out on the street and kept walking.

She did not know how far she walked and was not aware of her surroundings until she overheard some people speaking in Latvian. The language of the home-land extricated her from her stupor. She approached them. She asked if they knew of any place where she could take shelter. They directed her to a large attic room in a nearby building where many other refugees were sitting around the walls. There were no beds and no furniture.

She was there a couple nights before the leaders of the city arranged shelter for the refugees and dispersed them around the town. Momma ended up in a small village about two miles away with a farm family who had agreed to give her a place to stay. On the way there, she recognized the road and an overpass from a dream she had had while they were still in Berlin. She felt that this was the place God had chosen to shelter her and Jurit. Encouraged, she felt a wave of hope that he would get well.

Three generations of this farm family lived together: grandparents, their son and his wife, and their two children. Herbert was about 14 and Gisele, Laura's age. Momma said that thinking back to that time, she marveled how God had led them to a family that was not only willing to shelter and feed them, but whose kindness and empathy helped heal her heart. A few days after they arrived there, Andrit was born. The grandmother gave her baby clothes and diapers and every-thing else she needed.

The farm family had a cow and various other livestock so they had plenty of food and served it up in five meals a day. Momma said that rest and good food brought back her strength. She was able to walk into town frequently to visit Jurit in the hospital. She also did what she could to help out. One thing she could do was milk the cow. Since she had only one pair of shoes, she would go into the barn barefoot. She would then wash her feet by the pump in the yard before going back to the house with the pail of milk. Many years later after Germany was reunited, we set out to find that family to thank them for their generosity and kindness. The older family members were gone, but Herbert remembered the young Latvian mother who had stayed with them at the end of the War and who washed her feet at the pump after milking the cow.

It was more than six weeks later when Jurit came home from the hospital. He was quite weak and could barely stand. Momma said the fine soups and other good food the grandmother prepared helped him recover. Although Momma's German was limited, she often sat with the grandmother while they peeled pota-toes or did other household tasks. She slowly learned their family history:

The grandmother had come to the household as a very young woman to take care of a tiny infant and four older children, whose mother had just died. Their father had a lot of farm work to do and needed someone to care for his family. She became very attached to them and ended up marrying the widower. Together, they had the one son who now lived with them. The youngest of the older five never knew his own mother so she felt as if he was also her son.

That boy had been drafted into the German army and was serving as a medic on the Eastern front. She was very concerned about him because she had not received any mail in a couple months. Momma told her about Papa and the two of them talked about their loved ones and hoped that they would be reunited. Momma said the grandmother was very sympathetic and would notice what was needed and do small kindnesses on a daily basis. Momma said for the first time since leaving Latvia she felt safe. She wished that she would not have to leave them. But when the War ended, refugees were being gathered by the American Army. Displaced people were moved west away from the Russian Army that now occupied part of Germany.

When Momma parted from her warm-hearted hosts, they gave her a baby buggy and more baby clothes. There were hugs and kisses all around. Momma told me that each year when April rolled around she would think of them and wonder how their lives were going. But she could not communicate with them because their town was in East Germany and controlled by the Communists. Eventually after many moves among displaced persons camps in Germany and then the move to America, she lost the slip of paper with their name and address on it.

In June of 1945, all the refugees in the area were put on trains to be moved west to the American sector. The trains were open cars to start with (later they were moved to enclosed ones with the doors left open). The trip that might have taken a day or two ordinarily took three weeks. The tracks were destroyed in many places and troop trains and trains carrying supplies and food had priority. So their train would start and stop often. They ate cold canned foods. One day after eating pork and beans—rich food that no one was used to—many people got sick. The train had to stop by a small river. Everyone got out to bathe and to wash their clothes and diapers.

On another day when it started to drizzle, Momma remembered sitting against a wall and pulling the cover down over Andrit in his buggy. Momma, slumped back with her eyes half closed, noticed Jurit curled up on the floor and realized that she had absolutely nothing to cover him with. A Latvian man she had talked to earlier got up quietly, took off his coat, and covered the sleeping boy.

When they reached their destination, their housing was a partially bombed army barracks facility. The refugees would be housed in the part that was still standing. They were told to wait outside until rooms could be assigned. Momma sat down against a tree in the warm sun and allowed Andrit to nurse. She saw that Jurit, who had just turned six, was with a group of somewhat older girls chatting and playing so she felt safe enough to doze off.

All of a sudden she felt a hand on her shoulder shaking her. She started awake, but no one was there. Immediately the thought came to her to look for Jurit. She put Andrit in the buggy and drove it to where the little girls were gathered, but they knew nothing about Jurit's whereabouts. The buildings were nearby but she felt pressured to go in the opposite direction. In the open field she could see no sign of Jurit, but, as if a hand were guiding her, she hurried across it anyway. Then she saw the ground level swimming pool.

She moved as fast as she could and was horrified to see little Jurit in the water clinging to a piece of wood and gasping for breath. She grabbed him by his coat and pulled him out, but she doesn't remember that moment, just that he was suddenly on dry ground. Jurit had seen a colored box in the pool full of floating debris and was trying to get it out with a stick when he lost his balance and fell in!

Momma's heart pounded as she wondered how much longer Jurit, who was not able to swim, could have clung to that board with all his clothes soaking wet. Momma said this was another example of God protecting them even when they were least able to do anything for themselves.

As days and weeks passed, they settled into life in the camp which involved standing in line to get food and bedding and soap and other basic necessities of life. They shared one room; each room had a small coal stove that vented out the window for warmth and boiling water and warming food.

Although she had received no word from Papa, she did not feel that he was dead. She prayed about him every day and had a sense that he was out there somewhere. She kept hoping that she would hear from him and that they could be reunited. But months passed and she heard nothing. She submitted her name to the Red Cross and understood that they were trying to reunite families. But there was no news. She wondered whether she had made the right decision when she left Latvia and wondered what would happen to her if she ended up alone with two small children far away from her homeland.

At that point, people were still able to travel around Europe—even to areas controlled by the Communists; they would always take letters with them. So she was able to send some letters to her mother in Latvia to let her know where they were and that they were okay. The hardest thing was telling Mimite that Laura had died.

More months passed. Winter arrived. There was still no word from Papa. She had nothing to give her children for the approaching Christmas and often felt sad. Andrit, eight months old, had a fluff of white blond hair topping his small face. He could sit up and smiled often, but he was weak after recovering from a bout of whooping cough. Momma wondered whether he would ever know his father. Jurit was separated from the love of his grandparents and aunts and uncles and cousins. His sister had died. Now his father was missing. But in spite of all her worries, Momma trusted God to protect them.

When Papa found them on Christmas Eve, Momma did not recognize him (he was much thinner and completely covered in coal dust) until he smiled. Whenever they got to this part of the story they hesitated, as if remembering it was still too emotional. Papa always said all he ever wanted for that Christmas or any subsequent Christmas was his family.

Momma remembered arranging a bath for him. She took his clothes to be incinerated; they were full of lice. Other people living on her floor donated pieces of clothing so that he could dress in clean attire for the first time in months. Papa remembered sleeping in a clean warm bed.

Over the years, I had Momma tell her story many times and would remind her if she left out a part. She always said there was so much to be grateful for even though living through a War was horrible. They never starved and were never abused. At the same time she asked herself why God had chosen to send them so far from the homeland and so far away from everything familiar and dear to them. She was saddened that her children never knew the benefits of the circle of family and friends that were left behind in the homeland.

She would point out to me that many decisions they had to make were made in a manner of hours—sometimes minutes—yet the effects lasted forever. Leaving the homeland was a decision that she often thought over. She compared it to a time when her own mother was alone with small children during the First World War. Momma told us:

> *For a time, Russian soldiers occupied our house, but they were kind and behaved well. I remember one playing a mandolin and singing about his family far away.*
>
> *After the Russians retreated and the Germans advanced, we would hear stories that the German soldiers were savages and would do terrible things to women and children in their path. Mimite became fearful when streams of people came by the house on their way to Russia. They told her she should flee while she could. She*

hitched up Milda to a wagon and for three days did not unhitch her. Her father had written and told her to stay put, that no good could come of traveling with small children without any certainty about food or shelter.

When it started to rain, Mimite realized that her father was right. Heading out on the road with little Marta, Albert, and me was foolish. So she unhitched the horse and put her back in the barn and went to bed. Not much later the German Army arrived. Some officers commandeered most of the Inn, but left several rooms for Mimite and us children.

Marta would get snacks from the soldiers. One time she ate so much that she got sick. A German medic gave Mimite medicine and indicated on the clock when she should give it to her. Marta recovered nicely. The soldiers were always polite and caused us no harm. Eventually they went away when the War ended. They left behind a fine large copper kettle that the family used for cooking for years to come.

Momma said at least in the First World War civilians were not targeted and could usually stay out of harm's way. Now everything had changed and everywhere you turned there were more unspeakable cruelties being committed by one group against another. But in the end she said she realized that there was a purpose for their exile to a country so far away. "If we had not come to America, Papa would not have gotten the kinds of jobs he had, and we could not have afforded to help our relatives as much as we have. We have been able to do a lot to make their lives easier." For this, Momma was very grateful.

Duksit and Parsla

By the time I was almost eleven, Jurit had been on his own for more than two years. After he graduated from high school, he signed up to start college at a nearby two-year school. When he changed his mind and decided not to go, our parents were very unhappy. Papa especially could not understand why he did not want to further his education.

I remember a late evening argument when I was supposed to be in bed, but cracked the door to see and hear them arguing in the kitchen. Papa shouted at Jurit, "Do you want to work in gas stations all your life?" Jurit held his ground and soon thereafter he packed up and went to Omaha where he stayed with the Briedis family for the winter. The whole family was sad and upset. Jurit had been like an extra parent, always the organizer of games and excursions.

When I was about eight, he let me sit on his lap and drive his old Ford around the field. I just steered while he worked the gears and the pedals, but it was a magnificent feeling of power over a big machine that I have never forgotten. He taught us all how to handle the family's 22 rifle. We fired it off at some tin cans and bottles set up on a rock pile. I think he was the only one who hit anything, but the noise of breaking glass at a distance and the subsequent inspection of the damage that a gun can cause was impressive. He showed us how to clean the rifle. He said we must never ever touch it unless he or Papa gave permission.

Papa used it to shoot rodents in the garden. Once he shot a fox that wandered into the yard in the middle of the day. It seemed fearless and was acting strangely. Papa said it was sick and might have rabies. So he shot it, then picked it up with a shovel, carried it away, and buried it. We were told not to go near the spot where the fox had fallen.

With Jurit gone, we were left to our own devices. I think Andrit felt the void more than Max and I did because Max and I were always together and now Andrit was by himself. I think Andrit felt more secure in the company of his older brother. Once Jurit left, Andrit seemed to become more isolated. Jurit was always very competent and could fix his car and the farm machinery. Papa deferred to him regarding automobile maintenance.

While Jurit could talk to anyone out in the world and seemed very comfortable doing that, Andrit was shy and hesitant in dealing with strangers or new situations. Both brothers looked and were very different. Jurit had thick, curly, dark hair and a sturdy build. Andrit, whose hair bleached almost white in the summers, was slight. Where Jurit was active doing things, Andrit was observant. More often than not, he was in the house reading or drawing, rather than outside participating.

Although I noticed that the family had changed and that no one seemed happy, I had no ideas about how to make things better. So I spent more time with the animals and more time reading and more time daydreaming.

After the winter in Nebraska with the Breidises, Jurit joined the Air Force. He came home briefly before leaving for Texas and basic training, after which, he went to a Mississippi base where he saw a warm-weather beach for the first time. He took pictures and wrote letters about how nice it was with the palm trees and the ocean and how he liked the whole ambiance.

My parents relaxed and the mood of the family lifted because Jurit seemed to be doing well and making his own way in the world. Whenever he came home on leave, we were very excited to spend time with him. He took us to movies and provided our first meal at McDonald's. I still remember my first hamburger and my thought that it was the best thing I had ever tasted. The milkshake that went with it was indescribable.

My reaction to the fact that my brothers were going to grow up and leave home was to plan how to acquire more animals. We had several, but given the unreliability of their life spans, I believed more was better. The campaign to get a pony was going nowhere. Momma said, "If one of your brothers was interested, it would be different." Ostensibly a bigger, stronger boy could deal with a pony. But Jurit had left home and neither Andrit nor Max had much interest in animals in general—none at all in horses.

Where I got the idea to get a lamb, I don't remember, but a classmate who lived on a farm had a flock of sheep. So I talked Momma into driving out there to try to buy one. The summer I was ten we made the trip and looked over the herd. But Momma said they were already too big and too wild and all had their tails docked. So we made a deal with the owners that they would pick out a young lamb the following spring and not dock its tail and we would buy it around the age of six-eight weeks so it could be bottle-fed. Presumably, it would then grow up tame and easy to handle.

On the first of January 1961, I was the first one up and on my way to the barn. I knew that the older people had stayed up late to bring in the New Year. I had not, so I planned to feed the animals so that Momma could sleep in. I was anxious to prove that I could be dependable and would take care of the lamb as I had promised. I was looking forward to the new addition sometime in April.

Even with plenty of snow on the ground and snowdrifts where the wind had done its work, the path to the barn was still passable. A chilly wind drove small clouds of snow along the ground. As I got closer I saw something against a drift near the barn door that stopped me in my tracks.

Duksit was lying against the drift, partially covered by blowing snow. The wind ruffled his exposed fur. I knew he was dead. When I got closer, I saw drops of blood here and there and brushed the snow from his side. Behind his left shoulder was a hole with dark crusted blood in his fur. I tried to move a paw, but it was stiff.

I followed the drops of blood to the road and down the road to a large pool of blood, partially covered by snow, next to car tracks also covered over. It appeared that the car had stopped and then moved on. I ran inside and told the family. I think everyone came outside, but I remember mostly that Papa carried Duksit behind the barn and buried him in a big snowdrift, put some boards over him, and then piled a lot more snow on top of the boards. He said the snow drifts lasted the longest back there and in the spring he would bury Duksit properly.

I kept asking, "Who could have shot poor Duksit so close to his own yard? Why would someone do that?" Momma said that he liked to chase cars along the front of our yard and maybe someone who didn't like that did it. Years later I heard stories about teenage city boys who would drink beer and drive around the country shooting dogs and cats and sometimes larger animals. But that day I wondered if one of our neighbors could be the killer. People in South Dakota would not behave this way, I thought; clearly this was a very different place.

No tears came that day, but one night soon after I woke up crying in my sleep. I had dreamed about South Dakota and the Christopherson farm. Zimala, Tippy, Spolite, and Duksit were all there, glossy and well fed. I was so very happy to see them … and then I woke up. The dream recurred for many years and more animal ghosts joined the group, but the joyful setting was always the farm in South Dakota.

After Duksit died there were many discussions about him and dogs in general. One day Momma said that she and Papa thought it best that we not get any more dogs. I could not argue with their logic. Keeping them safe would require that they be penned or tied up and they were never happy with those options. Sometimes, after he had come back from roaming, we would tie up Duksit. His house was next to a small building next to the barn; from there he could see the whole yard. He would lie down at the end of his chain and look sadly at the activity in the yard. He would not bark or show any animation. When we approached with his food dish, he would sweep his tail back and forth slowly across the ground and seemed to ask, "What have I done to deserve this?" Momma could not stand the mournful display for more than a few days and would always let him go free.

Then he was back to clearing the yard of poultry when Papa came home and following us all around the yard and the fields. He had started to show some age since he was about eight years old. But he still had plenty of spirit and was always willing to show his affection.

While Duksit did his best to please the family, Parsla's goal was to please herself first and then to look after her cow family. After Zimala died, Parsla became the leader. Where Zimala was compliant and willing to accept that a fence—even one that was falling over—was to be respected, Parsla thought that any fence was a mere hindrance, an obstacle to be overcome. No fence would keep her from better grass, an alfalfa field, or the sweet corn in the garden.

When we first moved to the farm, vestigial barbed-wire fences marked off the borders of the property and the field near the barn that had been a cow pasture. Parsla just climbed through the fence oblivious to the barbed wire. After several such occasions (she had cut her udder and her legs), my parents decided that they should put up a different kind of barrier. Because the labor and cost of building a wooden fence was prohibitive, they decided to install an electric fence which, I think, their Latvian farmer friends had recommended.

They installed a small transformer device in the barn; an insulated wire led outside to the posts. Plastic insulators were slipped over thin metal posts and then a strand of bare wire was strung all around the pasture. Although the current provided an unpleasant sting (I know, because I got many such stings inadvertently when crawling under the fence or assuming it was turned off), it did no real harm. A plastic handle with a spring in it and a hook at the other end stretched the wire so that it caught a loop and formed a gate wherever you wanted one to be.

The fence needed regular maintenance because if too much vegetation touched it, the power would drain and pretty soon Parsla would know it and would break out again. Also deer tended to run through it and tear it apart. So every few days we would make a circuit of the pasture, cut down anything touching the fence, and repair any breaks. It was simple to do the job, so it fell to us kids to look after it.

In the early summer when the new calves were let out into the pasture, we took them out on a rope and halter and let them touch the fence so they would know to stay away. Otherwise they would run right through it. I always flinched when they invariably reached over to sniff the wire and got zapped right in the nose. But that was usually enough to keep them away and inside the pasture.

For Parsla, the electric fence was an interesting challenge. She got zapped a few times before she believed it was for real; then she stood and looked at it and raised her head to sniff the sweet corn just a few feet away in the garden.

Brownie and the young stock kept a safe distance away and were even reluctant to come through the gate by the barn for a few days until they got used to the idea that there was an opening and it was safe to come in when we called them. Parsla, of course, was fearless. It was apparent what she was thinking. She would look at the garden and look at the fence and then she would stomp away, whipping her tail back and forth, and march down to the pond pushing the other cattle out of her way

Not much later, I noticed that Parsla would graze closer and closer to the fence and then start reaching under the fence until the hairs on her neck just barely touched the wire. If there was a strong current, she would feel a tingle and then she would back away. When it became apparent that she would always test the fence, we had to be vigilant in maintaining it.

One early morning we heard Momma exclaim that the cows were in the garden. We ran out. As soon as Brownie saw us, she slunk back into the pasture. But Parsla, whose mouth was stuffed with sweet corn, just kept pulling more cobs off the stalks. As she greedily tried to stuff more into her mouth and others fell out, I grabbed the switch and smacked her on the hip to get her to leave. Rather than walking down the garden rows and out the other end, she stomped diagonally across the garden, crushing tomatoes, cucumbers and bean plants along the way while chewing her sweet corn!

The first few years that we were on the farm, Parsla had calves in the summer. Once, when she was missing for three days (Papa eventually found her in the deepest part of the swamp with her tiny offspring), he arranged for her calves to be born in the late winter. While Brownie accepted the fact that humans would raise her calves, Parsla did not. Even though they were reunited after the calves were weaned, Parsla was always outraged and complained bitterly when we did not allow her to nurse them.

Even when her calves were weaned, Parsla would sidle up to them and try to get them to nurse out in the field. One year, when her plan worked with a bull calf, Parsla was drained of her milk long before milking time. When Momma figured out what was going on, the little calf ended up spending the summer in the barn.

Late in the summer, when the hay was harvested from the far pasture, the cows were allowed to trek through the woods to the lush second crop of clover, timothy, and other tasty grasses. It was a large field and for the most part Parsla was satisfied. She did not try to get off our property, even though the fence surrounding the other forty acres was not particularly sturdy; some of it ran through a swamp, which was the real barrier to any wandering cattle.

As the days grew shorter and the fall weather cooler, Parsla's milk supply dropped off. She did not feel like hiking home so that Brownie could be milked. She also knew that the electric fence would be closed to keep them closer to the barn for the night. She started leading her family into brush and hiding when we came to drive them home. In response to that tactic, we fitted her with a bell on a wide leather strap around her neck.

Parsla learned to hold her head very still so that the bell would not ring. We put the bell on Brownie instead! We spent many hours looking for them and getting them home. Parsla was obstinate. Even as she got older, there was no mellowing of her nature. When my brothers had left home and I was going off to college, my parents decided that two cows were too much work. They gave Parsla, who was 16 years old at the time, to some friends who still had a small milking herd.

I finally got my pony when I was 17. Momma gave me a horse for my high school graduation present. I had horses for five years and many fine memories: learning to ride and learning to take care of the real, instead of the imaginary, horses. Two sheep lived on the farm until they died at the ages of 13 and 11. When I graduated from college and decided to go to Law School, I knew that I could not take care of the animals because my career would take up most of my time. So we sold the horses and gave the pony away. Eventually, we sold Brownie's last offspring, at the age of thirteen (Branga had been retired for several years). The cow family that had been with us for 36 years since we bought Zimala was gone.

Andrit painted the barn (its roof has been replaced several times), fitted new windows, and made various other repairs. The barn still stores the tractor and other implements and lots of split wood for the furnace. But whenever I walk inside, I still see the animals' faces turning to look at me, waiting expectantly for the snack I usually brought along. It was many years before I could go to the barn and not feel a pang at the absence of all the four-footed ones who had lived there.

Epiphanies

When I was about twelve, I met a girl in my class who had her own horse, a Tennessee walking horse. When she had it trained, she planned to show it and she was hoping to win prizes. She invited me to come and see it. One day I rode home with her on the school bus. Momma would come and get me later.

The horse was beautiful—a rich brown color with all white socks and a white blaze down his face. Since he was young, he was not trained to ride yet, but she worked with him every day. After admiring the horse, I asked to see her barn (I was always interested in all the animals that a farm harbored).

We walked in. It was milking time. I was dismayed to see the cows in their stanchions. Momma had pointed out to me how cruel stanchions are, how they caused the cows' shoulders to bow out as they reached down to eat, and eventually became deformed.

Each cow's space was very small; there was a sense of stress about the barn, quite different from our barn. It was easy for me to tell by that point in my life when cows were comfortable and well fed. I thought to myself that when I grew up I would do something to change such poor treatment of cows.

As I was thinking about this situation, my friend's father came down the line to hook up another milking machine. When my friend introduced me to her father, he nodded and kept working. Although I usually paid close attention to animals and how they looked and acted, I rarely noticed what people wore or how they had their hair or what kinds of clothes they wore. But that day I noticed how gnarled her father's hands were and how stooped over he was as he walked. He looked so tired. Later I asked my friend how old her father was. When she told me, I realized he was not much older than Papa. Later that evening I kept thinking about what a hard life he must have and although his cows were not cared for properly, in my opinion, no one seemed to be easing his burden either.

For some time Andrit had been scoffing at the books I chose to read, telling me that I should read some real literature instead of just animal and adventure stories. So that fall when I started the seventh grade, I asked him to suggest something that I should read. Although I don't remember the other books on the list he gave me, I did read two that had a profound effect on my view of the world.

I read *The Grapes of Wrath* by John Steinbeck and *The Good Earth* by Pearl Buck. Although I had long heard about war and the dreadful situations that war brings, I had believed that war is an anomaly of human behavior, that when war ends, things would always be getting better. These books changed my thinking. Many people all around the world lead hard lives where every day is a struggle just to survive. Realizing that these struggles occur even when there is no war to create difficulties, I think, was what made me start thinking about a career where I would be able to help people. I had no idea what that work would be, but I started to give it some thought.

Papa's mother Maria Ozols (right) with her parents/siblings c. 1908

Papa with his high school graduating class, back row right.
(Riga Latvia 1928)

Momma and her sister Austra c. 1921

Mimite, Ernina and Martina before the war

Grandmother Mimite (left) with her sisters c. 1930s

Ernina and her sister Austra in Latvia

Papa with a big fish, Latvia

Momma in the back row with her father Andrejs Kalnins.
Aunt Austra holds Laura and Jurit sits between family friends in Latvia
(1944)

Mimite with her daughters
(clockwise) Momma, Ernina, Marta and Austra

My parents in Latvia before the war (1939)

My parents' wedding (1938)

My parents and Jurit hike in Bavaria. (1949)

A scene in Germany.

Jurit and Andrit, Bremenhaven, Germany (1951)

Papa, Andrit and Max   Momma and Max
                                    in Germany

Max joins the family in Wurzburg.

Uncle Arvids in the Latvian cavalry

Sunday morning on Center Street, Vermillion (1952)

Max helps Andrit

Jurit and a carp

Jurit and Greta

Jurit and Andrit in the backyard of the house on Center St.

The cabin in the woods (winter 1955–56)

The Christopherson farm, South Dakota

Mr. and Mrs. Collar with us in Vermillion

The house on Center St.

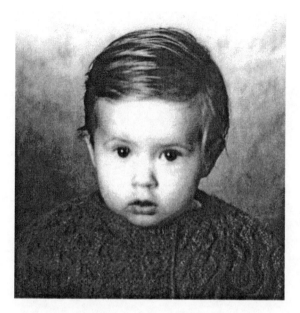

Ina arrives in NYC. (June 1951)

Brunite in her last years

Ernina visits South Dakota.

Ina and Max meet doggy

Ina helps Aunt Ernina milk Zimala (1954)

Ina, Janis Briedis and Zimala

Ernina and Ina in the boat, Max in the background

Momma at a lake in South Dakota

Ina, Momma, Ernina and Max before the drought set in

Andrit, Ina, Ernina and Max with Duksits.

Jurit and his siblings

Ina and one of the many calves
born at the farm on Spring Rd.

Ina and
Duksit

Ina and Mintz

Ina and rabbit
Vermillion, SD (1952)

Max and Ina and a turkey (1953)

Max, Ina and Jurit with rabbits

Ina and male turkey

Ina and Tippy
Christopherson farm (1953)

Ina, Zimala and Mintz (1954)

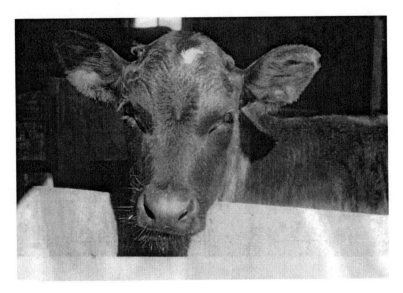

Parsla

The snapping turtle—South Dakota

The toys have a party and invite Ina.

Jurit's first car

Papa and Jurit with Teddy

Jurit reads the Bible to us.

Ina and Ernina

Uncle Rainits

Papa, Andrit and Max's girls burn rubbish

Papa on his pond

Papa, Andrit and one of the farm cats c. 1971

Momma and Papa with Max's family, Andrit in the back c.1980

Max and Jurit

Anna and Laura (Max's daughters) visit Wisconsin

Papa and Wisconsin sunflowers

Momma and Papa (mid 1980s)

Momma's 68th birthday (October 1983)

My parents in Florida

My parents' place in Florida

The grandchildren (in front from left) Anna, Laura, Robert and Brian
Cathy, Max, Momma, Papa, Andrit and Ginger (1980)

Ina in her office

1986

By the summer of my 36th year, relationships with Eastern Europe had thawed. It was now possible to travel to the homeland. If you went with a group, travel arrangements were easier. Momma had learned about such possibilities from her Latvian friends. She was eager to make the trip but she did not want to go alone. Papa believed that as long as the communists were in control of Latvia, it would not be safe for him to return. Momma did not press him.

So that summer I set aside my three-week vacation, cleared my calendar (rescheduled court appearances and reduced the number of cases I took at my job as an attorney in the Wisconsin Public Defender's office), and planned the trip. I got a passport. Momma obtained her citizenship so she could also get a passport. We were just about ready to buy our tickets when bad news startled us. The nuclear power plant accident at Chernobyl gave us pause since we did not know what effect it would have on the Baltic States. Reluctantly, we decided to put off the trip.

I suggested that we take a road trip instead, since I had already set aside my vacation time. A trip to Colorado to visit Max and his family would be an option. We could stop in Omaha to visit the Briedis family on the way home. Papa, 75, and Momma, 70, liked the fact that I was volunteering to do most of the driving. When we headed west, the day was hot. After one stop, in western Nebraska for the night, we arrived in Glenwood Springs the following day. Max's daughters, Anna and Laura, were 15 and 14 and of an age where trips to the mall and the pizza parlor were easy entertainment.

One day the girls suggested that we hike up a nearby mountain to a vantage point they thought I would like. Not being used to the altitude and after having to climb over numerous fallen trees to get there, I was exhausted. The view was striking but I told them that I did not know if I had the energy to get back down. They said, "Oh, there's a shorter easier route." There was a clear trail back to their house!

Max and Cathy lived in a house on the property of the owner; in exchange for paying no rent, they acted as caretakers. Because they also had other jobs in town, they were always busy. Having become very skilled at fly fishing, Max did find time to hike into the hills to fish for trout; their freezer was full of trout that he had caught.

After about ten days with Max and his family, we drove along to Denver where they had things to do and then parted company. On the way home we stopped in Omaha and visited the Briedis family for five days. My parents had not gotten together with them in a long time so they all chatted nonstop whenever they were awake. I spent some time with one of their youngest daughters who had been born after they came to America. Her husband, who was learning Latvian, already had quite a vocabulary.

As we continued homeward, my parents suggested that we swing by Vermillion since I had never been back once we left in 1955. They had been back several times; on one occasion, they brought Mrs. Collar back to our farm where she spent the summer. By then the judge had died and she was in a nursing home. Although she was crippled with arthritis, mentally she was fine. Gracious and grateful she told Momma many times how much she appreciated the holiday from the nursing home. The parents had planned to send her home on a plane, but the airline would not take someone who could not walk. So they drove her home. We never saw her again. Her condition deteriorated and she died a few years after that visit.

I was very curious to see South Dakota and wondered what I would think of it. It was a hot July day when we drove in to Vermillion. The streets were wide with large trees overhanging them. Everything was covered with the flat dusty light of a late summer day. Not much traffic and few people seemed out and about. Momma had no trouble finding the small house on Center Street. The outside was unchanged. Although the lawn was mowed, it did not look like anyone lived there. No flowers, no garden, and no signs of humans. The entire street was very quiet; there were no sounds of kids or dogs.

We walked around and looked at the backyard. I took pictures. I looked over the fence at the Collar house and that was quiet too. I remembered Max hollering out "goodbye my sweetheart" and the wonderful sound of Mrs. Collar's laughter. Our old house was locked; the windows had curtains so we could not see inside. After a quiet period with our thoughts, Momma suggested that we drive out to the country to see the other places where we had lived.

Momma directed me to the Star Prairie School which looked like it had been closed a long time because trees were growing through the wooden steps in front. The windows were nailed shut with boards. All around brush and weeds grew very tall. We drove by Helen's farm where we had spent the first winter in the country. It looked like a working farm. In every direction were flat fields of corn and other crops.

A short distance farther on, Momma warned me not to miss the turn. I had trouble spotting a driveway but was able to pull in a short distance. I couldn't understand why we had stopped. Momma said we should get out because this was the Christopherson farm. I would never have recognized it. Everything was overgrown with brush and brambles and small trees. We could see the house and some of the other buildings, but because the vegetation was chest high, it was going to be hard to get closer. As we debated whether it would be worth the effort, a man on a tractor pulled in behind us.

As soon as he said *hello*, we recognized Harry Scholtens. He said he had come by because he wondered who could be stopping at the old farm and once he recognized my parents he wanted to talk to them so they talked for quite a while. He said that he and his father had bought the place and farmed the land. They raised crops but kept no animals. As they visited I looked around and what I remembered as a valley leading to the little creek now looked like an overgrown ditch with brush and a few scraggly trees along its edges.

There were no signs of the flower beds my mother tended or the mulberry bushes that Papa had trimmed. There was no lawn where we had played with Tippy and Duksit and rested in the shade of large trees. The driveway that allowed for the arrival of our cars and Mr. Christopherson's pickup was impassable. It was also very quiet with just the breeze rustling the dried weeds. No animal voices talked to each other. It was desolate and abandoned and the sight was wrenching.

Harry told us that no one had lived on the farm in many years and that they had made no effort to keep the house up. He also told us where Helen lived in town with her daughter and that she would enjoy a visit from us he was sure. After exchanging addresses we drove back to Vermillion and found Helen at home. Her health was failing but the friendly voice and demeanor was very familiar. While my parents visited with her I struggled with the emotions that buffeted me—there was nothing left of the farm and the time that I remembered.

We left in the early evening and I drove until I got tired and then we found a motel. The next day we got home and I thought to myself how green and lovely Wisconsin was even in the heat of the summer. After dropping off my parents I went to my home in a small town about 25 miles away and started getting organized in order to go back to work. I kept thinking about those early years in South Dakota and that seeing how things were now I had lost something again but I wasn't sure what. My subconscious must have sorted all that out because after that trip I stopped dreaming about South Dakota.

Return to the Homeland

By midsummer of 1987, Momma and I had made our plans, bought tickets, and packed and packed. Momma wanted to take as many clothes and other items as she could so that her siblings could either use or sell them. Shoes, very hard to find in Latvia at that time, were always in demand.

It was not possible to fly directly to Riga, but there were two alternatives. One route: fly to Moscow and then back 500 miles on a Russian airliner to Riga. The other: fly to Helsinki, Finland, take a boat to Estonia, and then a bus along the coast to Riga. Momma opted for the latter plan and signed up with a group tour that was familiar with this track.

In anticipation of our trip, Momma communicated regularly with Ernina who sent money (she wanted Momma to deliver this money to the other siblings). In addition to Ernina, by that time in our lives, we had met one other relative, Uncle Arvids, Momma's oldest brother. He had traveled to America in the late summer of 1976 even though it had taken him six months and several trips to Moscow before he could get the paperwork he needed to leave the country! He was 70 years old that year. Russia was permitting older people, not considered important to the Communist effort, to travel abroad.

When Uncle Arvids came to visit us, Ernina came down from Canada and traveled with my parents and Arvids to Denver to visit Andrit and Max and his family. They also visited Jurit and his family in Minneapolis. Arvids stayed for six months (the maximum time allowed by both governments). He even traveled to Florida with my parents before flying home again.

Momma was very excited about the impending trip. I was looking forward to meeting the rest of Momma's siblings and cousins that I had never seen. About four days before we were scheduled to leave, a ringing telephone awakened me at about five o'clock one morning. (In my line of work such early phone calls always meant trouble.) As I answered, I wondered what bad event was waiting on the other end of the line.

Momma's voice was breaking as she told me that Canadian authorities had called to tell her that Ernina had been found dead in her apartment! She had fallen, hit her head, and bled profusely. Whether she had had a stroke or a heart attack, they did not know. She was 76 years old and they did not suspect any foul play. In her papers, they had found Momma's name; neighbors had confirmed that Ernina had a sister in America.

Momma and Andrit were flying out that morning to Montreal to deal with things. We were all in shock. I could not think what advice to give her. I told Andrit to call me collect when they arrived in Canada so that we could talk about what to do. The rest of that day was spent in a fog. I had not seen Ernina in several years because she no longer felt able to make the long trip to America. I had not made the effort to go to see her. I had told myself that I would do it next year ...

After several phone calls back and forth, I suggested that Momma ask the Canadian authorities whether they would hold her body in the morgue until we got back from our trip to Latvia. We could then drive up there and make all the necessary arrangements. They agreed, so Momma and Andrit flew home again. A day later we left for the trip to the homeland.

The flight was a blur. I don't remember much until the morning after our arrival in Helsinki, an interesting city. We walked around a little bit before breakfast so that we could find some bananas (bananas were rarely available in Latvia) for Aunt Marta who loved them. Then we gathered for the bus ride to the boat which was large and comfortable. It was a beautiful day. I walked all around the deck to look at the Baltic Sea, smooth and blue as far as I could see. We had lunch on the boat and after about five hours docked in Tallin, Estonia.

Although there was no visible curtain between the free world and Estonia, there might as well have been. The most noticeable thing was how gray and soot-covered everything was. The customs workers all seemed tired and grim. When we got through customs, we loaded our baggage on buses and set off for the trip south along the Baltic Coast.

Given the convoluted route we had to take, I thought to myself that the Communists must want to be convinced that we really want to get to Riga. The tour guide told us it would be a ten-hour trip on the bus. We did stop for dinner at an obviously ancient resort, right on the seashore, which gave us a lovely view of the ocean. The guide, a young Latvian woman, chattered nonstop when she wasn't leading the group in Latvian folksongs, all the way to Riga.

About ten o'clock that night we reached the outskirts of the city. At that time of the summer, it was still quite light out so it was not hard to see how gray and deteriorated the buildings were. Momma exclaimed in a soft voice over and over how sad everything looked. Nothing at all like the city she remembered before the War.

The buses pulled into a covered driveway next to the Hotel Latvia, a relatively new building that rose over 20 stories in the heart of Riga. The Hotel Latvia was the only place tourists were allowed to stay and our guide reminded us of that several times. *We were not allowed to stay overnight with relatives and must always return to the hotel.*

Around the bus, a large group of people were waiting for the arrival of relatives. I recognized Uncle Rainits from pictures, but it was obvious that although Momma was just a couple feet away from him, he did not recognize her. I stayed back to allow them some space for their first meeting after more than 43 years. He was holding a bouquet of flowers.

They spotted each other almost simultaneously. Rainits kept saying, "Olgina, you look so old, you look so old." Although she had sent many pictures over the years, in his mind she was still as young and beautiful as she was when he last saw her. Martina, Momma's sister, was also there. After hugs and kisses and tears all around, they agreed to wait for us in the park across the street until we had checked into our room.

By now, it was close to eleven at night. I had to check my watch to make sure because it was still light enough that you could easily see where you were going. Momma and I soon joined our relatives in the park. We visited with Momma's sister and brother and my cousin Ligita, Rainits' youngest child. Time and again the discussion came back to Ernina because she had made the trip to Riga earlier and had always kept in close contact with her siblings.

Momma had not yet told them that Ernina had died. After a while, I excused myself and said I was too tired and wanted to go back to our room. Once in the hotel, I went into the bathroom, ran water for a bath, and burst into tears that refused to end.

I couldn't bear the sight of Martina's and Rainits' happy expressions as they talked about how wonderful it would be if all the brothers and sisters could get together. "Next year in Riga we could all be together," Rainits repeated several times.

It was after midnight when Momma came to the room and told me that she had told them about Ernina. We soon fell into a deep sleep. By four in the morning it was light, and Momma was up soon after. We went to breakfast and then to the lobby where Martina was already waiting for us.

A couple days later we went to a memorial service that Martina had arranged at her church for Ernina. Most of the family was there as well as some old friends. Cousin Andris' oldest daughter played a moving violin solo. Everyone sang old Latvian hymns in the obviously neglected old church which seemed to envelop us with comfort. It must have witnessed many sorrows over the several hundred years that it had stood there. Paint peeled everywhere and the pews had deeply worn spots where worshippers had sat or rested their arms.

Martina told us that only old people went to church. Although religion was not totally forbidden, the government discouraged it. But that day those of us gathered there felt comforted. Every note and every word was clear and crisp; the acoustics were marvelous. Later I learned that the siblings had decided that Ernina's remains would be cremated and that Momma would bring them on her next trip. Ernina would be buried in the homeland.

We were mostly confined to Riga. One place we could travel, however, was to Sigulda where Rainits and his family lived. Martina, who knew the schedule and where to catch the train, went with us. We left in the morning with a suitcase of clothes and boots and shoes for the family. We spent the day there, joined by Uncle Arvids, who arrived on a train from another part of Latvia. It had been ten years since I had seen him; he had aged considerably. Momma had a pair of shoes that fit him perfectly which made him very happy. Aunt Austra, Momma's youngest sister, arrived in her own car which Ernina had helped her to buy. She lived on the other side of Riga, but we were not allowed to travel there.

Since we could not stay overnight, the visiting had to be cut short. We had to catch the last train back to Riga. Before we left, we made plans for everyone to gather in Riga in the next day or two. The siblings were all very glad to see Momma, but at the same time they were dealing with the loss of Ernina, so the gathering was muted. Back in the city, Martina walked us to our hotel. Because she lived only a few blocks away, we saw her every day. I gave my breakfast ticket to her so that she and Momma could visit over their food. I knew that the nine days of our visit would not be enough to catch up on all those years of separation.

One day Momma's youngest brother Rainits drove me around the city in his car and told me stories about his youth. He said when the Germans first occupied Latvia in 1941, he was gathered up and sent to a Hitler youth camp somewhere in Germany. He said it wasn't bad and involved lots of sports and hiking and marching around. After several months, he was allowed to return to Latvia. Then when he turned 18, he got a draft notice to report for induction into the German Army. He and a couple friends decided to ignore the notice.

A short time later he was arrested and sent to a jail which he described as "not a nice place." They were on a limited ration of food. From time to time the guards would knock them down and beat them. So when he was released after a couple months and told to report to the Army, he did so promptly.

He worked as a truck driver, shuttling supplies to the German front lines. On one such late-night mission, the first truck in line was blown up by a land mine and the whole convoy came to a halt. Suddenly, someone yanked open his door. Russian soldiers pulled him out. He was not armed and along with the other drivers they were marched to a building and taken down to a cellar. They were ordered to strip to their underwear. His hands shaking and body shivering, he did as he was directed. He thought he was going to be killed.

To his amazement and relief, the Russians brought in uniforms of their own and ordered them to get dressed. They told them they were now in the Russian Army! He finished out the War driving trucks for the Russians. But when the War was over, he was sent to a Russian prisoner-of-war camp, where he sat for 18 months. He said he saw many older men die because of the limited sanitation, and the scarcity of food.

After he was released, he returned to Sigulda in Latvia to work on a construction project for the government. There he met his wife. Eventually they had two children and they built the house where we all gathered for our recent visit. I asked him whether I could buy anything for him because most goods were very scarce. Only tourists could shop in the store connected to the hotel. The locals could go into the store only if accompanied by a tourist. The government wanted to get American dollars and this was another way that they could do it.

His tires were bald, he said, and he could really use some new ones. One day we went into the store and I bought new tires for him. Everything there was much more expensive than it would have been in America. The small boom box (which would cost $40 in America) cost $150, but I bought it for him because he loved music.

One afternoon I went for a walk around the city and stopped into a couple stores to see what was available. One announced that it was a "fish store." Inside an old woman swept a floor that she had probably swept several times already. Six cans of tuna sat on one shelf. There were numerous such examples. I asked my Uncle how people got their food.

He explained, "A lot of food falls off the backs of trucks as the trucks arrive. Most sales take place in the alley behind the store. Or, you stand in a line and then everyone buys all they are allowed of a certain item until it's all gone. It would be hard to survive without a garden and a pig or some chickens." He added, "Austra has a large garden and grows lots of potatoes and other root crops. In the fall, the city relatives come out to help her and bring her things from the city, like coffee, and she shares her harvest. She also has a cow and makes cheese and butter. Her siblings can always count on her largesse."

Although there were shortages of everything else, there was an abundance of flowers. Every time someone came to meet us or we went to visit someone, we were given armfuls of bouquets. We brought them back to our hotel room. The staff provided vases at first and eventually just glass jars. Every flat surface in the room held containers of flowers. Presenting flowers had always been a custom, but Momma thought it was even more extreme than when she lived there. I thought it must be a hunger for beauty because everything around them was gray and run down.

Much too soon our visit was over; we had to board the bus to make the return trip to Tallin. Martina took our departure the hardest. She waved at the side of the bus, started weeping, and then ran away. Momma had promised to come again, but just when we couldn't say. On the trip home, I wondered what my life would have been like if I had grown up in that circle of family and friends.

I know that Momma would have been happier, but I also wondered whether Momma had now traveled too far to ever really fit in again with her family. Momma had lived all those years in freedom and they had not. Their focus was on obtaining the basic necessities for survival. A close-knit group, they had shared many experiences and hardships. But they were all together. They helped one another. They could not imagine the heartache Momma had felt at being so far away. I mulled all this over, but had to acknowledge that I was much relieved when we boarded the boat for the trip back to Helsinki.

Wild Apples

In the late spring of 1992, my parents returned to the farm from their winter in Florida where they spent almost every winter since Papa retired. They had gone to visit Jurit and Ginger in the early seventies and were drawn to the sea and the warm weather. They loved the seacoast of their Baltic homeland, but they had not been on a beach since the summer of 1944. The year before Papa retired, they drove along the East coast of Florida and settled on a small town about half way down the peninsula. When they started looking for a property to buy, Jurit suggested a duplex. There would always be someone living in their house and the rent would help with the mortgage.

The one they found was rather neglected; it had been on the market for a while but was only half a mile from the ocean. Able to see its potential, they were pleased when they were able to buy it. They both loved the ocean and walked along the beach almost every day. They swam when it was warm enough and when the waves weren't too big. I knew all this because I had started spending my vacations with them in 1990.

One very warm April day, Papa got out the chain saw to cut up an apple tree that had fallen over during the winter. Later that night he had trouble breathing. Andrit drove him to the hospital where, after various tests, we learned that he had a badly calcified aortic valve that barely opened and closed. Without surgery, the doctor told us, very few people lived two years after such a diagnosis.

We were shocked. It seemed like Papa's health and strength had not diminished even though he was 81 years old. Papa did not struggle with the decision. He said he did not want to undergo surgery and would live whatever days God was going to give him. The doctors prescribed various medications. We took him home.

My parents had tickets for a trip to Latvia in a couple weeks and Papa said he was still planning to go. It was important that he see his homeland. When the Doctor asked him whether it was worth dying to make that trip, he said quietly "yes, it was". The news of Papa's condition reverberated through the family.

Jurit and Ginger brought their boys for a visit. Andrit and I drove our parents to Chicago so they could catch their plane. Now that Latvia was free again, they could get a direct flight to Riga via Copenhagen. At the check-in counter, the agent gave us a pass so that we could push Papa in a wheelchair right to the gate and sit with them while they waited to board. An airline staff person soon took them down the gangway and out of our sight. On the way home, Andrit and I wondered whether we would see Papa again. I could understand his wish to go home, but I dreaded the thought of them so far away if his condition worsened.

Two months later when they returned, we met them at Chicago's O'Hare. Although Papa, riding in a wheelchair, looked frail, he was quite chipper. Glad to be back, he was very glad to have gone to his homeland. Momma's brother Rain-its had driven them to all the old places. Papa even found a cousin he had never met before. The drive home involved lots of chatting until we got into Wisconsin when they both fell asleep in the back seat.

By fall, Papa had lost 40 pounds (he did not want to make his heart work any harder than it had to). His spirits were good, although he often stated that he couldn't do anything anymore and was not useful. We tried to reassure him that he did not need to do anything other than just visit with us. I told him that we still needed him and when we no longer needed him, we would tell him. I assured him that he would be the first to know when we reached that point. I told him that he could trust me because I was the family lawyer. He always laughed at my little joke.

He started to spend a lot of time reading (Andrit would get books from the library that he thought might be interesting to him). Andrit would also take him for rides in the car and would help him with his bath. When he wasn't reading, we would find him napping on the couch in the sunroom. Almost every day he walked down the hill to his pond where we had set up a lawn chair for him so that he could sit and watch the sunlight play on the water.

He had this pond built in a swampy area that was fed by a spring. It was much bigger than the one that was in the middle of the pasture. During its early years, they had lugged lots of plants and bushes to plant around its edge so that rain storms would not wash out the dam. By the fall of 1992, the wild things were reclaiming it. Cattails grew everywhere they could set their roots. Lily pads floated on the ripples. Weeds and brush choked off the rim, making it hard to walk around it. Andrit carved a path so that Papa could walk part way around if he wished, but mostly he liked to sit in his lawn chair.

Come November, they announced they wanted to go south again and we made our plans for the trip. Momma still did at least half of the driving. I did all the heavy lifting. When we arrived in Florida, I got the phone hooked up, noti-fied the power company, and brought home the heavy groceries. I trimmed the palm trees and tried to anticipate what might be helpful to do before I left them on their own. After they were settled in and rested from the trip, I flew home.

Our family had a new regimen. Momma seemed to have no trouble adjusting to Papa's not being able to do any major physical tasks. They did go to the beach almost every day, but now they drove rather than walk the half mile as they had done for so many years. Papa sat and read or just looked at the ocean and Momma went for her walks alone.

The next summer Momma went to the homeland on her own and was gone for almost two months. Andrit and I could tell that Papa missed her more than ever, but he did not complain. We tried our best to keep him company and to cook dishes that he would like to eat. When we brought Momma home from Chicago, it was dark, but he was waiting up and came out on the steps. He could not stop smiling when he saw her.

In the fall, I drove them to Florida again and flew back down to pick them up in the spring. On the trip home, they told me they were both planning another trip to the homeland. I could not quarrel with their wishes even though I feared the effects of another such trip. Papa just said it was all in God's hands.

When we picked them up again two months later at O'Hare, Papa seemed smaller and very tired. He said it was a good trip and he was glad that he went. During the two years after his diagnosis Max and Jurit and their families came to visit—usually at different times—most often in the summer. Papa was always glad to see them. My parents' place in Florida was far from all their children, but as the days grew shorter they started talking about heading south again. They seemed to hunger for the warmth of that seacoast.

After our return to the farm in the late spring of 1995, Momma said she wanted to travel to the homeland again. Would I go with her? Her last remaining brother Rainits had been in and out of the hospital with heart problems. Her older brother Arvids had died a few years earlier after suffering a stroke and her brother Albert had died in 1936 from complications of appendicitis. So we made our plans to be gone for about three weeks.

Riga had undergone major changes since I had seen it seven years earlier. Everywhere you looked, scaffolding was set up and buildings were being repaired and painted. Dozens of little restaurants had sprung up as well as all kinds of shops and stores. I learned to my dismay that my camcorder battery charger needed a special adaptor to fit the outlets at our hotel. I went out to see if there was any place nearby that I could buy one. A couple blocks from the hotel there was an electronics store that had everything I needed.

Many more cars were on the street and many newer foreign cars. There was also an energy in the air that was lacking during my first visit. The Riga market, which stretched for blocks at the edge of Old Riga, had every kind of food item you could imagine. Aunt Marta, who had spent a year and a half in America, including a winter in Florida with my parents, had been to visit us twice. She took me on hikes around the city to show me the improvements and pointed out that Riga now had a McDonald's.

We visited Rainits at the hospital in Sigulda where he seemed to be doing fine. He came outside to sit with us in the hospital garden. He said that some tests were being done and that he had to stay while they observed him. Then he laughed. I taped everyone and everything on my camcorder so that I could show them to Andrit and Papa when I came home.

Toward the end of our trip Anton, a first cousin to Papa whom we had never met, called us. He came to our hotel after we agreed to meet him. Papa had found a first cousin during one of his trips. Anton had heard from that first cousin about Papa's visits which prompted his call to us. We had a long chat. I filmed most of it so that I could show it to Papa. I was struck by the similarities in Anton's expressions and gestures.

His father and Papa's mother were siblings. Anton said that the family had always wondered what happened to Papa and whether he survived the War. Papa, who had felt that they were not interested in him, never made any attempt to find out about them after the War. Anton, who became a close friend, was always available during Momma's subsequent visits to accompany her around the city and to help in any way that he could.

Having met one of Papa's relatives I spent more time thinking about what our life would have been like had we been able to grow up in Latvia—if there had been no War and if Papa had stayed at the university. Momma said she had envisioned a life where she spent the summers at the seashore with the children and winters in an apartment in the city. Papa would probably have become a professor at the university since he was doing very well there.

There would have been lots of visits with relatives and large gatherings for holidays and birthdays. They would all have doted on me and I might have become spoiled. That trip I learned that Aunt Austra also made wonderful tortes. One warm afternoon we visited her farm and had a feast of torte and a huge bowl of steamed fava beans. Neighbors and our Russian chauffeur (who worked at the hotel and had driven us out there) and the mail lady sat outside around a picnic table. Although there were some language barriers, they did not affect the festivities. Aunt Marta and a neighbor had a little wine and sang Latvian folk songs. I helped open the beans and I always encouraged the cake to make its way around the table.

Everywhere we went I would find myself thinking about the lives my parents had lived and the struggles of starting over in a new country. I realized that the character they brought with them made a great difference to the life of the family. My parents had plenty of arguments. Papa had a temper and sometimes seemed to blow up over small things. As they got older they seemed to spend more time than was necessary bickering over minor things. But all that became small stuff as I grew older and saw them more clearly. They did not crave toys or expensive clothes or excitement of any kind. During their life together, they bought only two new cars which they drove down to the last mile. Whenever they could, they fixed old things rather than throw them away.

The polestar of their lives was their very strong faith in God and the teachings of the Bible. Momma often said faith had guided their every step; the more difficult life became, the more she learned to rely on that faith. Papa would agree. Then Momma smiled and pointed out: "We came to America with a few boxes of odds and ends. If we ever had to move from the farm on Spring Road we would need a train!" She said that God had given us far more than we needed.

In early August, we flew home to a very warm summer. Day after day it was hot and sticky. I went back to work. Aunt Marta, whom we brought back for her third trip to the USA, stayed on the farm. Later that month Max and his entire family drove in from Colorado to visit. Jurit's oldest son Brian came over as well. His younger brother Bob had been there earlier in the summer and was now in D.C. where he served in the Air Force.

The last day that I saw Papa was a Sunday and we all had a big meal. Papa did not eat much (he had been eating less and less in recent weeks) and said he had no appetite. I can't remember why, but we needed to multiply several three-digit numbers and no one had a calculator. Papa came up with the answer in a few seconds. Although he was frail, he was still mentally sharp and I would reflect on that example of his acuity later.

As I was leaving, I told him not to walk me to the car as was his habit because it was dark and there was no need for him to do it. But as I got to my car door, I felt him near me and he gave me a very strong hug. He was very warm and later I would think that he was like a candle flaring before going out. I would also realize that he was saying goodbye. At the time, I couldn't see it. I kissed him and said I would be back the next weekend.

Later that week Max's oldest daughter, Anna, drove to the airport in Milwaukee to pick up her husband so that he could meet Papa. Max and his wife, Cathy, packed up and went to Waukesha to visit her parents before heading home to Colorado. Max forgot his suit and Aunt Marta said that was a sign that he would be coming back soon.

On the last day of August, Martina and Papa sang some Latvian folksongs. Momma and Andrit said he was in a very good mood. The weather had broken and it was a crisp fall-like day. He put on his gray fleece jacket which he liked because it was warm and very light. His thinning gray hair and long silvery beard (he stopped shaving after he retired) blended well with the color of the jacket. He told them that he was going to walk down to the pond. Momma said, "If you go that far, pick some wild apples from my favorite tree."

Andrit said that from where he was working in the garden, he saw Papa heading down the hill. Later he saw him stop and zip up his jacket and start up the hill. When it seemed that he should have made it up the hill, Andrit went down the path to look for him. He found Papa halfway up the hill crumpled on the ground, still breathing but unconscious. Andrit ran up to the house to call for emergency assistance. The ambulance, which was there in a few minutes, drove out to the pasture, close to where Papa was lying.

It was all to no avail. Papa died on the way to the hospital. By the time Andrit called me, they were home again. I went to my house where my nieces and their husbands had gathered, as Anna and Judd had just driven up from Milwaukee. Laura and Jeremiah were there too. We were in a daze. I had the thought that if we just didn't go to the farm maybe it wouldn't be true.

The next few days were a blur of notifying friends and family and making arrangements. Beautiful flowers came to the farm; cards and letters and phone calls gave everyone something to do. Neighbors stopped by with food. I suggested that Max give the eulogy. I didn't know who else would be able to do it.

After the ceremony in the funeral home and the graveside ceremony, we gathered at the farm for food. Max's girls had made all sorts of things in anticipation of the guests. It startled and pleased me to see all the old friends who came and talked about Papa.

It also startled me how every small comment and friendly pat on the shoulder moved me. Whenever I was alone I could not stop crying, but I would gather myself when I was around Momma. I stayed with her day and night for a few days and slept in her room. She did not sleep much and it was hard to see her so crushed. She said that she had gotten so used to him napping on the couch in the sunroom or reading there that she thought their life together would just go on forever.

Over the next few days, our family parted again. Max and his family drove back to Colorado, Jurit, Ginger and Brian back to Minneapolis. Bob was the last to leave when we took him to the local airport for his flight back to D.C.

Momma told me later that about a week after everyone left, she was sitting in their room looking out the window at the lovely view. She thought about how Papa liked to look out over the fields and the woods. She thought about some of their last conversations about their lives and how they had come to live in this wonderful place.

Papa told her that he was very grateful for the life that God had granted him and that he had one last hope. He told her that he prayed often that he would leave this world without great suffering. She was warmed by the thought that his prayer had been answered and his last wish granted. He had slipped away so quickly.

She couldn't motivate herself to do anything until she noticed the brown paper bag that the hospital gave her containing Papa's clothes and other personal items. The bag was on one of the chests that Papa had made for the trip to America. Seeing it there, she felt a need to deal with his things. She unrolled the edge and folded it open. She took out his watch and his wallet and a comb. The shirt that they had cut off him while trying to resuscitate him was also in the bag.

At the bottom of the sack was his favorite gray jacket that he had worn that last day. When she got a grip on the soft fleece, she pulled it out of the bag and noticed that it was heavier than it ought to be. She lifted it and checked the pockets. They were filled with sweet wild apples.

978-0-595-47842-2
0-595-47842-5

CPSIA information can be obtained
at www.ICGtesting.com
Printed in the USA
LVOW08s1630250417
532132LV00002B/170/P